# THE GREAT BRITISH RAILWAY STATION

# EUSTON

### K.J. ELLAWAY

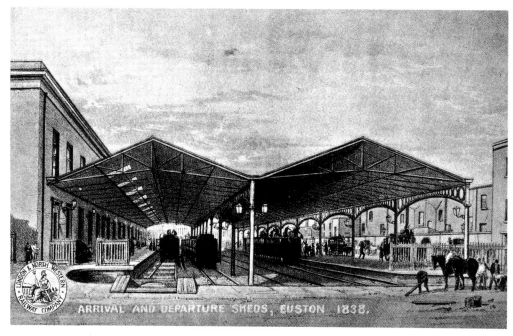

*'Olde Euston' in 1838 - the station nearly ended up at Camden Town but the London & Birmingham pushed on to "Euston Grove". One inducement was that the land in between would soon be covered in buildings and any chance of a (cheap) nearer approach "altogether lost". The land moreover would be got on "comparatively favourable terms" whilst another factor was the hope and expectation that other companies would use the route conjointly - principally the Great Western.*

*Copyright Irwell Press 1994*
*ISBN 1-871608-28-7*
*Irwell Press,*
*15 Lovers Lane,*
*Grasscroft,*
*OLDHAM OL4 4DP.*

*Masterpiece amongst propylaea. This was the great sentinel marking the London & Birmingham's "Euston Extension", in suitably dramatic style. At over 70 feet it was higher even than its progenitor, the inspirational entrance to the Acropolis in Greece.*

*Printed by Amadeus Press, Huddersfield.*

# CONTENTS

*Acknowledgements*
*A number of brains and some extraordinarily vivid memories were tapped for this account- in particular Alec Swain, John Wiseman, Siegfried Becket, I.C. Coleford, John Hooper, Ian Sixsmith, G. Reeve and Chris Hawkins. My thanks.*

*The Great Arch under a louring sky, June 1945. Shrapnel gouges could still be seen up and along the Euston Road, at the bases of many of the buildings - well into the 'sixties at least.*

# CHAPTER ONE
# ANCIENT GREECE TO PREMIER LINE

Unique if only for an exalted status as 'the headquarters and principal terminus of the greatest railway undertaking in the country,' Euston nevertheless seldom aspired to any temple of the great. The London and North Western Railway itself was painfully aware of this fall from grace, how this greatest endeavour of the Empire, the London to Birmingham Railway, had lost its classical edifice 'the fountainhead of the LNWR's whole vast system' in a collection of scruffy streets remote from any obviously respectable part of the capital.

First authorised as early as 1833 the London and Birmingham opened some five years later; in the days when 'London ended at Marble Arch'* the first section opened from Euston Square to Boxmoor (later Hemel Hempstead) on Thursday 20th July 1837, trains departing the London terminus at 10am, 2pm, 5pm and 7pm. 'Box Moor' departures were at 8am, 12 noon, 4pm and 6.30pm (after Scott, *The London and Birmingham Railway Through Harrow*, Borough of Harrow, 1987). A full service to Birmingham began on 17th September the following year, 1838. Euston thus came into being as Victoria ascended the throne. Amongst the

nicest accounts is that of S.M. Phillip (it is spelt Phillp but I take it to be Phillip) in *The Railway Magazine* of January 1900. The magazine in their early years attracted many histories penned by senior railway officers – they had a 'PR' justification for the time expended, and unique access to railway records. Such accounts are invaluable for their 'contemporary' feel and a joy for the language used. Presumably a railway officer was one of those few not deemed certifiable on expressing an interest in railway origins.

*The Railway Magazine* was also a fine platform to loose off a few rounds – bemoaning the 'congested and narrow thoroughfares' by which the great station must needs be approached. Phillip (or Phillp) declares this to be 'an old story, with which students of the history of early railway enterprise are tolerably familiar; and Euston affords a striking illustration of the want of forethought displayed by the legislators of a past generation.' (Such sentiments have a disturbing resonance, given the subsequent fate of the Euston Arch). Its gestation was more halting than might be appreciated; 'Euston' indeed might easily have never come to such universal rail-

way fame ('What London is in the World of Cities, Euston is amongst Railway Stations' is how *The Railway and Travel Monthly* put it in 1911) and the site for the proposed London and Birmingham terminus was moved tentatively about north and north west London. The railway, wherever it ended up, would not be able to pierce the built up perimeter set by Parliament, the mechanism which gave us our ring of termini and was so railed against in *The Railway Magazine* of January 1900:

*The promoters of railways in those early days had an up-hill task in contending against the forces of ignorance and prejudice, especially on the part of landowners, whose property they had to acquire; and one result of this was that in constructing their terminal stations, particularly in London, they were debarred from approaching the sacred precincts of the City and West End, and the 'accursed thing' was rigidly kept at a distance on what were then almost the outskirts of civilization. Thus we find the London and North Western at Euston, the Great Northern in the wilds of Pentonville and the Great Western at Paddington.*

*H.P. White Regional History, London, D&C 1963, 1971.

*Patriot 4-6-0 at Euston on 12th December 1938, No.5532 ILLUSTRIOUS. The graceful curves of Euston were evidenced intermittently as shafts of light battled with the steam and smoke underneath. Beyond is the old No.1 or 'bell' box. Photograph H.C. Casserley.*

*LNW 2-4-0 No.276 PLUTO (withdrawn in 1907) according to the description on the print, on the Euston departure plat-forms. By the 1890s outgoing traffic had long outgrown the accommodation provided for it. Trains, whether local or long distance, were taken out by long shunts on arrival, marshalled and sent back into the platform roads on the outgoing side. "Starting away for the return journey from the same platform as that into which the train had come had never been enforced at Euston" the Station Master complained in 1902. Photograph by arrangement John Tatchell.*

*Philip Hardwick's Doric Arch (it cost the astonishing sum of £35,000 at the time, a measure of the effect the Directors wished to make, "to stand for all time...") in period splendour. The gilded EUSTON was inscribed in 1870. Photograph by arrangement John Tatchell.*

Jackson (*London's Termini*, D&C 1969) lists as candidates for the London and Birmingham's capital terminus sites in Islington (Regents Canal) and at Marble Arch, followed by one at Maiden Lane (of Kings Cross fame). Phillip keeps its simpler noting 'the original terminus' which it was intended to make at Chalk Farm – there followed, prior to opening, an extension to Euston, then known as 'Euston Grove'. The Camden Town idea arose from Parliamentary proposals of 1833; these were successful and followed a rejection of the Maiden Lane notions the previous year. Here is some form of *rationale* of the 'Euston Grove' extension, a long letter (signature indecipherable, but presumably an L & B Officer) to the Board of Directors, dated 7th February 1835. It demonstrates as well as anything the precise circumstances behind 'the last leg' of the L&B, into Euston. Today's Department of the Environment might care to learn something from the costing principles, put forward probably for the first time in history:

### London and Birmingham Railway

Assuming that the extension line is intended to be exclusively for the conveyance of passengers and that the goods carried by the Railway are to be received and delivered at the Camden Town Station, the Annual Receipts for the additional mile to Euston Grove would according to the Estimates submitted to Parliament be only £5,754.18s.0d, a sum which it is obvious would not afford any adequate compensation for the necessary expense of making and maintaining the Railway: but as the Returns from which these Estimates were framed do not comprise passengers to and from places short of Edgware, a large addition should be made to this number for the intermediate distance.

The principle of all calculations of traffic in passengers by Railways is that the numbers will be in proportion to the superiority in 'cheapness, certainty and expedition' of this mode of conveyance over Road travelling – Now it is clear that by bringing the Railway a mile nearer to the centre of the metropolis (by which 7 minutes of time will be gained on each journey) there will be an additional superiority in these requisites, and that a proportional increase in numbers may consequently be assumed. This increase whatever it may be should be a set off against the first cost of the extension line.

To a person who has a journey of 100 miles to make it may be an object of little moment whether it shall occupy 5 hours or 4 hours and 53 minutes – (although even in this case it will be a positive accommodation to him to be spared a mile of road on his arrival or departure in addition to this distance by the Railway) but when the journey is not to exceed 10 or 20 miles the saving of time becomes important especially as it will occur on that part of the line where a saving will be the most desirable.

At the ordinary rate of Railway travelling the journey to Watford and back, a distance of 30 miles, will require an hour and a half – fourteen minutes of time and a Turnpike saved with 2 miles left of Road to go over will in this case have an influence which those can best appreciate who are in the habit of witnessing the importance attached to such savings by persons whose business carries them daily into London. The mere circumstance of the access to the Railway being in so frequented a thoroughfare as the New Road will decide many to resort to it on excursions of pleasure who would never exert themselves to go a mile out of the way for the same object. No where is it more important that places of resort, whether for business or amusement, should be conveniently situated than in London, and the comparative convenience in this respect of the Stations at Camden Town or Euston Grove can scarcely by disputed. It would be vain to attempt any estimate of the general increase of traffic from the proposed extension where the data on which it should be founded are so insufficient, but considering that every person who may be induced from the additional accommodation thus afforded to the public to go upon the Railway for a distance of ten miles will be equivalent to ten persons on a single mile, it is not unreasonable to anticipate that the return to the Company will be sufficient to compensate the outlay – An average increase of numbers which should be equal for the whole distance of 112 miles to 70 Passengers daily, would at the rate of 1d net per passenger per mile produce £11,965 or 10 per cent on the estimate.

In considering the merits of this question it should not be forgotten First, that if the decision of the question be adjourned to another Session the open ground through which the Railway is to be carried may be then covered with Buildings and the opportunity of making it on comparatively favourable terms be altogether lost.

Secondly, that should this Company neglect the opportunity so offered to them others may possess themselves of the proposed line of approach.

Thirdly, that considerations of convenience will induce other Companies to make use of the London and Birmingham Railway for the Approach to the Metropolis and that the charge to this Company will be thereby proportionately reduced.

Finally, that a nearer approach to London was a part of the original plan in the Session when the Bill was thrown out and only abandoned from the difficulty of making the Subscriptions on the contract Deed equal to the necessary estimates, and that the present line presents fewer obstacles to the Engineer, and is much less expensive than the line to Maiden Lane.

It has been suggested with reference to the expense of the additional mile of Railway, and to the great accommodation it will afford to Passengers that power should be taken for a higher rate of toll in the Amended Act – The policy of a Clause to this effect, unless intended for the purposes of prohibition as respects other Companies, is very questionable – Looking to the benefits which steam Packets are reaping from the low price system, and also to the fact that the more the passengers who are conveyed by any one Engine upon the Railway, the less will be the average expense of power upon the whole numbers conveyed, there does appear to be every inducement to make the change for passengers at the lowest possible remuneration rate with a view to attract the greatest number – There can in effect be no doubt that the success of this plan could be at least as efficacious with the Railway as it has proved with Steam Vessels and Omnibuses.

**7th February 1835**

The arguments were compelling, more or less; the extension had already been agreed and a contract for the work was made on 25th November 1835, with William and Lewis Cubitt, who were later to play such a role in the completion of the Great Northern and Kings Cross. The London and Birmingham agreed (in something termed the 'Euston Square Extension Contract') that the Cubitts should 'make a part of the railway from Drummond Street to a point about ten yards north of the Regent's Canal in the parish of St. Pancras.' It amounted to £76,860 and the Cubitts were responsible for maintenance for one year after completion. Some of the material excavated was to 'be carried over the canal' and would form the embankment for 'the Chalk Farm Depot.' The spoil would also form part of the site of 'the intended depot at Euston Grove.' Euston was indeed called many things in its long existence but 'depot'? Never, surely. 'The stratum of ballast' for the new line should *be beaten into a firm and solid mass by heavy beaters worked by at least two men and the thickness before mentioned shall be considered to apply only after this operation has been effectively performed. Upon this surface the blocks or sleepers are to be laid in their proper situations for receiving the rails, when stone blocks are used each block should be bedded in its proper situation by frequently lifting it by a spring lever to the height of one foot above the surface of the ground and letting it fall forcibly on the ballasting, this operation shall be continued until no sensible difference of level is perceived after each fall. Should the block then be found too low it shall be removed and more material placed on its intended bed and the above operation repeated until the block has reached its proper level and has*

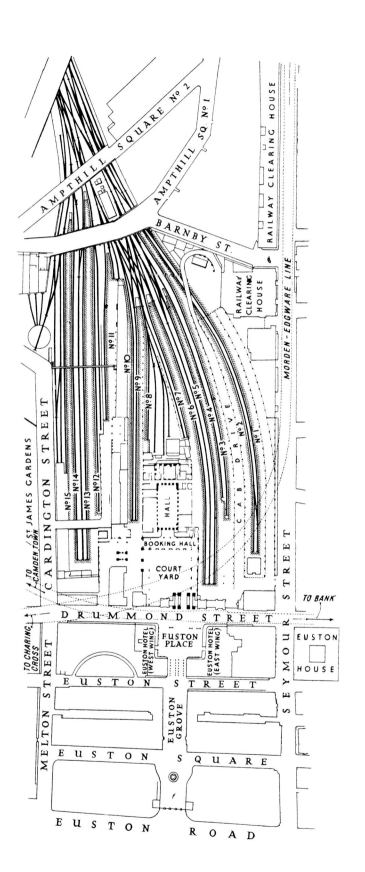

46154 THE HUSSAR *enters platform one, summer 1954 with 'the Ulster Express'. Photograph G.W.Sharpe.*

*Left- Euston 1938, courtesey The Railway Gazette. Opposite - 'Old Euston' 1838.*

*Euston as she was - a period of relative calm, a mixture of stock, intermittently punctuated by the barking report of some unseen engine, blasting out to an echoing roll of noise and smoke, typified the place. Oerlikon stock forming a Watford local and 2P 40683 on a Northampton arrival, 27th July 1957. Photograph collection Brian Morrison.*

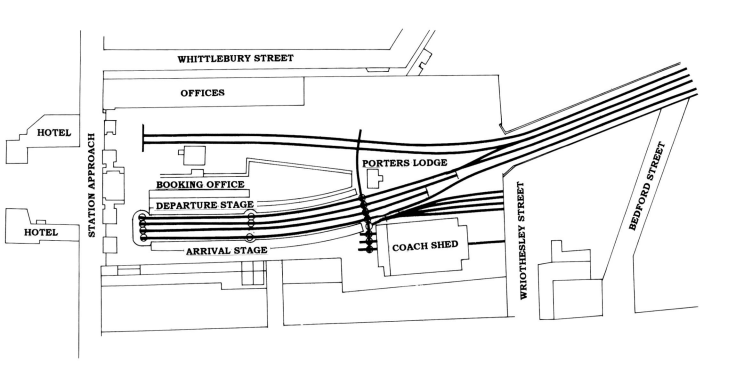

*Euston Station Hotel, 15th December 1954. There could certainly be few stations like unto Euston, and the call, that "London is to cities what Euston is to stations" was very true. Station and streets about merged almost imperceptibly in a glorious warren, melding age, style and, to a great extent, the varying degrees of dereliction. The two Euston Hotels were the first in the world, the 'Victoria' on the west side and the 'Euston' on the east, the latter the better class establishment. This is the linking building put up in 1881 in the "modern French style" by J. Maclaren and so deplored by Alan A. Jackson in his book 'London's Termini'.*

obtained as firm and uniform a bed as can be obtained throughout the whole area of the underside of the block.

There were four lines of rail on the Extension: *...the two outside lines of way are to be six feet apart, the two inside twelve feet apart and the distance from inside to outside of the rails of each way is to be four feet eight inches and a half apart. The stone blocks will be delivered to the contractors in their rough state and they will be required to drill two symmetrical holes in each block six inches deep and two inches in diameter, to make the upper surface in each block perfectly level, and to drive the oak trenails and cut off their tops flush with the surface of the blocks.*

There was also much talk of wood sleepers so the way was not by any means made exclusively of stone blocks. The work, it was agreed, would be complete 'on or before the first day of January, which will be in the year of our Lord one thousand eight hundred and thirty seven.' The Extension Contract did not include the station itself; this was arranged the following year, 1836. On 7th December an agreement was signed for 'the erection of offices, entrance portico, lodges, gates and other erections and buildings in the intended depot or station at Euston Grove.' The contract specified almost every tiny detail, such as the panelled ceiling of the portico, to be formed, it declared, 'with double laths and mastick cement, collared and jointed to resemble as nearly as possible the stone used in the portico.' The Cubitts again took on the job; it included office buildings, first floor

and ground floor (the place was now beginning to be termed 'Euston Grove Station') and refers to a 'station keeper's dwelling' among other things. The cost of construction for 'Euston Grove' came to £39,850.

The extension down to Euston Grove had left the London and Birmingham with a pronounced dip, an inconvenience laying just exactly at its London end. For some years it operated very much after the fashion of all afterthoughts, which of course is was, through an ever more complicated arrangement of cable, brakesmen and so on. 'The business end' in terms of goods and chattels and the locomotive operating part was at Camden. The steep 1 in 68 and 1 in 77 grade was considered inappropriate for steam engines though in the first few weeks banked trains, that is with engines at front and rear, had to be used, until the system of cable was installed and working.

Jackson gives a fine technical account of the bank, which gave rise to its own specialist operations. Tickets were collected at Chalk Farm and trains sent down to Euston, attached to the cable and under the control of 'Bankriders' – dashing chaps who saw that the speed did not exceed 10 mph or was lower in suitable instances, such as a train of excessive weight or if the Rails were '...in bad order'. A bizarre signalling system involving policemen with flags and an organ pipe using compressed air, further ensured safety. *The Railway Fly Sheet and Official Gazette*, a respected if irreverent trade paper put it thus in October 1879:

In 1831-32 the London and Birmingham Railway was projected, and the metropolitan terminus was then at Chalk Farm. After great opposition, a Bill was carried in 1835 for bringing the terminus to Euston Grove as it was then termed. But the public were yet timid of the dreaded locomotive coming into their midst, and the fear of boiler explosions and other evils prevailed, so that until the year 1845 the engines came no nearer to London than Chalk Farm, where they were detached from the trains, and from thence the carriages ran down into Euston Station attached to a break, and were worked back by means of rope moved by a stationary engine at the Chalk Farm end of the line.

Amongst the most ancient and dignified (at least it once was) of our *Great British Stations*, Euston was accordingly laid out in eccentric fashion; it was moreover curiously lopsided. In keeping with early practice an arrival and departure side sufficed for all workings at first but they were offset to the east of the great portico and its lodges, the space to the west side, which would have made for a wholly more symmetrical arrangement, languishing for want of the Great Western. There had been talk of that company sharing Euston Grove but the broad gauge, it seems, could not be accommodated (the GWR would have connected with the L&B at Kensal Green). This mattered not, in the sense that the L&B, and later the LNWR, required in the end all the space it could get, but in this early hiccup we can see already the seeds of subsequent confusion at Euston. As it was, at first the station must have presented a remarkable and stirring sight. Rising out of ordinary fields, ditches and lanes at the straggling edges of the city (the gas works, brick fields and pox hospital must have been visible down the road at Kings Cross – see *The Great British Railway Station: Kings Cross*, Irwell Press, 1990) was this vast *propylaeum*, bigger even than its Athenian antecedents. The locals, a sorry lot, must have marvelled at it, forming the principal point of a screen some 100 yards in length, the noble arch flanked by blank sided vault-like buildings inadequately term 'lodges'.

It was fashionable to compare this lengthy Athenian assemblage to the other north London termini, though it is a much lesser known contrasting than the familiar and obvious Kings Cross – St. Pancras. The Euston screen is matched in a number of contemporary texts with St. Pancras, usually to the latter's detriment. St Pancras was the haunt of 'costermongers and the lower classes' and had 'sprung up whole and complete', thus making a relative virtue of Euston's *ad hoc* accretionary nature. The home of The Premier Line was as far removed from high Gothic as it was possible to be; it was 'like Aladdin's Palace.'

There were four 'lodges', one joined each to the side of the Euston Arch (which we shall call it from hereon – *propylaeum* and *portico* are fine terms but the Euston Arch is forever the symbol of the station, as much for its loss as anything else) and two more set apart to the east and west. This was Philip Hardwick's Doric masterpiece. Robert Stephenson had planned the Euston Grove terminus and Hardwick had been the architect. Hardwick's son was later responsible for The Great Hall. Euston grew, true enough, 'hideously and chaotically' (H.P. White, *Regional History*, D&C) and so did the streets around it. After long years condemned literally to the back streets of architecture and town planning, the Arch and Hall were torn down and thrown away. The Arch it would seem, by its passing, was assured of more affection than ever it appeared to have enjoyed in its long years closeted amongst mean, inferior buildings, ever blackening in the London air.

"No one visits railway stations to look at architecture," James Scott declares in *The Fascination of Railway Stations\* and then proceeds to more or less eulogise over the Arch and the grandeur of the thing. He regretted the hurrying passengers unheeding of the Arch's beauty and blamed in particular the covers of Hackney coaches and taxi cabs, confining the range of one's vision. The glory of the Arch had in any event long been dimmed by lesser structures huddled too close. "It was ever a thing designed to stand in splendid isolation – the main entrance to the station should be seen by all who can appreciate fine structures. If they have an eye for beauty of curve and line, and purity of design, they will find in this Grecian propylaeum a structure which will gratify their sense of elegance."*

In these sentiments Scott was certainly right, though he spoke as something of an artist – the author of *Studies in Ideals,* no less. *The Railway Fly Sheet* of 1879 held less lofty sentiments; after all it was a business paper: "entry to the station is through a gateway beneath a lofty Doric arch. This has been the wonder of many, for though handsome in itself, and possibly one of the largest porticos in the world, its object or necessity cannot well be understood ..." The account puts its cost at 'about £30,000' and notes, unimpressed, the weight of some of the blocks used in the Arch's construction – up to 13 tons. Alterations were under way at the time of *The Fly's* prognostications; work 'lately commenced' in extending the wings of the hotel seemed to *The Fly* likely to hide the Arch from view (!) whilst 'rumours of its demolition are already afloat.'(!!)

*The Fly* liked the Great Hall better –

*The Railway and Travel Monthly, June 1911.*

"one of the best works of the late Philip Hardwick" it declared. Passengers passed into it from the Arch via a yard and doorway "at the fringe of the station's stir" and in 1879 it had been only recently redecorated – "a fitting introduction to the great iron thoroughfare of which it forms so dignified a threshold". The Great Hall had opened in 1849, a concourse and waiting room which, Jackson notes, provided a model for many big stations in the world. Otherwise known as 'The Vestibule' at the turn of the century, a hopelessly inappropriate term, the Hall was ill positioned either as a central feature (for it was slightly offset from the Arch) or an aid to future enlargement of the station; any development westward would leave the Hall awkwardly slap in the middle of things. The Hall certainly became something of a hidden treasure, tucked away in the cheap wrapping paper of subsequent decades. There were many doorways into the different parts of the station and its platforms and five doorways were let into the outer vestibule of the Great Hall:

A gallery runs round three sides of the hall, and the Board Room of the Company is reached by a flight of steps surmounted by a range of Doric columns, the sculptured groups being emblematical of the progress and industry of science. In the hall is a marble colossal statue of George Stephenson, and around the galleries are the various offices, tenanted daily by their hundreds of busy occupants, who transact the business of the company.

From its first simple departure and arrival platforms the station gradually groped its way to the east and west until it was contained within a rough rectangle, Drummond Street – Seymour Street – Cardington Street. Much of the expansion work dated from the late 1860s through to 1874, with another burst in the late 1880s – early 1890s. Parliamentary powers were obtained for the acquisition of additional property on the east side and additional roofing, two new and lengthy arrival platforms together with curved cab incline, making its own bridge over the lines. The various thoroughfares by which the station was approached were undeniably of mean character and under powers of 1869 a wide road was taken across the garden of Euston Square. This new approach from the Euston Road appeared with a bronze statue of Robert Stephenson and the two further 'lodges' bearing in gilt the name of all the towns and cities to be reached from Euston. Some (and they are there still) would have sailed fairly close to the winds of the Trades Descriptions Act. The delightful carriage shed had to go and in the same period what was surely one of the most peculiar station improvements to take place in this country well, took place – in a most peculiar fashion. *The Fly* again, of October 1879:

The aggregate length of platform for this terminus is upwards of a mile, and is divided into three arrival and two departure platforms. Euston differs from all other principal London Termini in its construction, which is really that of an

*The Arch, in the 1930s it would seem. The earlier wartime view, shorn of advertising, far better suited its dignified bearing. It was possible to ascend inside the Arch to the top, where, in a strong room, all the title deeds of the LNW were kept - arranged, classified and indexed, "in an appropriately musty atmosphere".*

7

*LNWR times (milk churns to right) at Platform 2. Photograph by arrangement John Tatchell.*

immense shed. It is said that there are not less than 8,980 square yards of glass in the skylights alone. The east side of the station was considerably improved a few years ago by means of a novel and ingenious contrivance.

The roof over the railway and platforms had for some time required a general repair, and having been erected many years ago, it was also found deficient in height, for ventilation, etc. Being 900 feet long and 140 feet wide, with light wrought iron principals at short distances, and covered with boarding, and slated, provided with light by skylights in the usual way, the question arose as to how the immense traffic was to be provided for during the alteration. The course was at length determined upon of raising the roof *bodily* in sections, by means of *screw jacks*, to an additional height of six feet.

The roof, as we have mentioned, was 140 feet span in five bays, varying in width from 40 feet, the widest, to 20 feet, the narrowest, carried upon cast iron columns rising 14 feet 6 inches from the platform level, which again were connected by light arched open cast iron girders about 20 feet long from column to column, 3 feet deep at the haunch. Upon these ran the gutters, and the principals spanned the space between the rows of columns. Five lengths of these spans collectively were to be raised at once, with their columns, to 6 feet above their original position, and then cast iron pedestals were to be inserted between the old base of the column thus lifted and its original foundation, thus giving the area to be dealt with, at one operation, as 140 feet wide in four spans, and 100 feet long; the process having to be repeated until the whole was raised.

Underneath the cap of each column was fixed a casting, bolted strongly together in 2 halves about 3 feet long, each end of which was supported upon an upright piece of timber about the height of the column – the false caps, thus supported, taking the whole weight of the roof. The two pieces of timber thus described were connected at the bottom

by timber, furnished with two cast iron 'boots', each of these boots prepared for the reception of the end of the screw or of a screw-jack. The whole of the roof was carefully tied with timber on each side of the principals, bolted together, the greatest care being taken, by the introduction of ties and struts, that the whole should be perfectly rigid. Diagonal braces were brought down from this timber framing to just above where the jacks worked, so that any chance of tipping or shifting was guarded against. At each angle, and at some points on the side, were fixed strong timber guides, up which the roof travelled, and which kept it securely in its place.

The whole structure being thus well secured together, and the jacks fixed in their place, the word of command was given, and the great area of 14,000 superficial feet, *columns and all*, was raised 'six turns of the screws,' about 6 inches. Accurately prepared wood gauges, with which the men had been provided, were then applied; and when all was ascertained to be correct, a second order was given, and the screws rose six turns more, when the next set of gauges were used; and the time occupied in lifting the whole mass 3 feet 2 inches high was only fifty minutes – the work having to be done at a slack time of day, in the intervals between the trains. And all this so thoroughly organised, that the traffic of the station continued as usual; and of course no portion was at any time exposed to the weather – the roof always continuing as an efficient protection.

The Directors of the London and Birmingham had decamped from premises at Cornhill in 1838, taking up residence at Euston and determining, in this flush of accomplishment, that a station hotel would be appropriate. *Two* were built, across Drummond Street, in 1840, labelled *Euston* and *Victoria*, and connected, with a certain whiff of Gothic, by a subway under the intervening courtyard. There remained, for a few years after this, until the hotels were joined in 1881, the vista of the

Arch from Euston Road. Once this had been shut off the station really was left to its 'cogerie of mean streets' and little that could be called inspirational happened thereafter. Jackson calls the period 'Adding Dreariness...'

A 'Granite Roadway' had been built from the first to divide off the eastern London and Birmingham side from the putative GWR western side. The latter's non-arrival meant the ground lay fallow for a while but the available space on the western side really came into it own in the 1880s, when sorely needed expansion took place. 'Euston Station Enlargement' begins life in the Archive as a list of costs, from December 1886. A vast undertaking indeed, its record runs through to June 30th 1892 and includes such items as diversion of Cardington Street (at the west side of the station – it was displaced even further to the west, across a burial ground), excavation and removal of human remains from St. James's burial ground £6,460; completing removal of human remains from St. James's, undertakers work in connection with the above in 1887, more cases and coffins in 1888, and lots of work on water and gas mains etc. The grim business of body transfer went on throughout, and the whole of the ground was probed at the end to ensure no unfortunates remained in unhallowed ground. As late as January 1891 three bodies were removed from the station works to Finchley, in new coffins.

In May 1891 several hundred pounds was expended on engine power in connection with the works, trains of spoil being conveyed to Willesden. The work was finished off with the construction of several girder bridge openings, under Ampthill Square and so on, 'for the new platform lines to be extended in a northerly direction.' This stage commenced in 1888 and involved the new platform roofing (by the latter part of 1891 the cost was put at £4,570), five additional platforms and booking offices at the southern end, with an independent approach from Drummond Street.

Unloading girders and materials for new signal box etc., engine power removing clay to Willesden, crane hire in May 1891 – the work ground on and must have rivalled the dust blown chaos of the final rebuilding in the 1960s. Another tranche of £6,390 was gobbled up in obviously a further consignment of ironwork in 1890, £570 for a new 'platform and horse landing,' £550 for new buffer stops for platform and west side incline, £58 on lots of tanks and water columns for engines, and £35.6s.11d. no less, on furniture and ticket cases for the new booking office, as work came to a close, in May 1892. The awesome total by June 30th 1892 'including liabilities' was put at £476,745.5s.8d.

All this had left Euston with an independent approach on the west side, though two separate entrances to the station was found to be unsatisfactory. 'It was therefore decided' to connect up all the new accommodation formed by the new platforms (12-15) with the main part of Euston by an extension of the cab yard, once more to the west, "which involved a large amount of work in supporting the office buildings overhead to suit the altered arrangements. A new booking office was provided in a better position to serve all the platforms and a real improvement effected in the working of the traffic" (*Euston, By One Who Knew It Well*). The old carriage shed was swept away in all this and was reconstituted in a more modern guise out at Willesden in 1888. In 1873 two timber platforms had appeared on the east side, Nos 1 and 2 'for the accommodation of local trains'; by the 1890s Euston was thus at its greatest extent in terms of platforms, Nos. 1 – 15, east to west.

'Old Euston', the station of steam days that is still remembered, really dates from this work of the 1880s – 1890s. The Board of Trade naturally had to have a look and the LNW wrote to the Board on 12th January 1891, describing the "proposed rearrangements about to be carried out between Euston and south end of Primrose Hill tunnel." The BOT, giving provisional sanction, noted that "the lines and junctions are numerous and intricate but the project appears to have been carefully worked out, the only defect that strikes one at present is that the engine shed is placed at one side and away from the lines on which the engines work, requiring nearly all the lines to be crossed by the engines instead of being in the middle of this work."

The LNWR proposed to bring "the new signal cabin which has been erected at this station" into use on Sunday 19th April 1891 and before that it had to be inspected:

**Provisional sanction was granted by the Department some months back for alterations in the lines and signals between Euston and the south end of the Primrose Hill tunnel, during the progress of the works which the company have in hand, but as the locking frame in the new cabin here is of unusually large size it is thought that the Officer to be appointed to inspect the works in question might like to examine the frame before it is made use of. Such inspection should take place on Friday next 17th instant. Company officers regret the notice is so short but they do not anticipate being ready for the inspection before Thursday afternoon and on Saturday it will be requisite to partially dismantle the frame to make some temporary alterations....**

Things did not proceed quite as well as expected; on Wednesday 15th April 1891 The Board noted that the LNWR now proposed to bring the new cabin apparatus into use on Sunday 26th, "instead of Sunday next, as was at first contemplated...." Major General Hutchinson duly inspected and subject to numerous alterations – all of a minor nature, errors in the arrangement of levers 197 and 198 and so on. Remedial work was duly carried out by 17th May the following year, 1892. The alterations on the east side too had been made ready:

*"I beg to state that the works carried out on the east side of the station are practically finished and might be inspected at any moment but very considerable alterations have, since the date of the inspector's visit, been made on the west side of the station which although not yet quite completed are so far advanced that I will ask you to be so good as to accept this letter as conveying the first notice of their fitness for inspection. The date upon which the whole of the works here can be submitted for inspection is so comparatively near to hand that I would venture to suggest for the consideration of the Board of Trade that the reinspection of the new signal cabin might be postponed a few weeks..."*

On 24th June 1892 very detailed diagrams were sent to Maj. Gen. Hutchinson, rendering it unnecessary, it was hoped, for him to work it all out on the ground. *"Having regard to the difficulties attendant upon an inspection during the daytime when the traffic here is in full swing Maj. Gen. Hutchinson was kind enough, I understand, to offer to pay a visit to Euston at midnight and I am to say that the company's officers have made such arrangements as will afford him the greatest facility in testing the locking at midnight on Tuesday next the 28th instant, if he can oblige us by making it convenient to come here at that time. I am further to state that it is proposed to open the new or western side of the station for public traffic on Friday next, the 1st July."* A further inspection a short time after that found arrangements satisfactory. On 29th July 1892 the company forward detailed

*More LNW times. Claughton 4-6-0 coming home. Photograph by arrangement John Tatchell.*

*The Premier Line could certainly put on a good show. Leading is Precursor 4-4-0 No.811 EXPRESS with Prince of Wales 4-6-0 No.979 W.M. THACKERAY behind. They became LMS 5311 and 5630 respectively.*

*drawings of the bridge carrying Hampstead Road and Ampthill Square over the railway lines, and final sanction for the whole episode was formally given in November 1892.*

Much of this work of the late 1880s through to the early part of the 1890s was contracted to Holme & King of Liverpool – £43,815 in one large contract "to complete the said works on or before 1st May 1889." All the inter-related jobs ran along quickly – this one was signed on 13th March 1888 for instance and comprised:

"(a) bridges under Ampthill Square, Hampstead Road, Granby Street and Stanhope Street and widening the railway on the western side of the present main lines etc.

(b) retaining walls culverts etc.

(c) restoring and new paving

(d) draining

(e) labour

(f) all temporary works including scaffolding etc.

Holme and King put in the turntable foundations at Euston, in 1890 (it was 54ft at first) but the period was marked by a series of complicated tenders; apart from Holme & King a large number of them went to Messrs. Kirk and Randall – they had at least five contracts, Messrs. Parnell another couple and various other concerns, including the Shap Granite Co. mopped up the rest of the work.

Jackson draws attention to a proposal at the end of the century for complete re-building of the station, indeed an Act was obtained for this end but it apparently sank quietly out of sight. Euston was in any event cursed by a highly restricted approach; by 1900 both fast and slow traffic out of the terminus down to Camden was worked over one up and one down line, and it became absolutely essential to provide for two additional main lines so that fast and slow traffic could be separated. To "prevent the increasing delay and difficulty involved by the fouling of the main lines, due to backing out of the empty trains from the arrival to the departure side or in sending the carriages to Willesden."

Powers were obtained in 1900 to widen the cutting out of the terminus, which included the purchase of property alongside. The permanent way required wholesale rearrangement, extra sidings were to be established together with new carriage sheds, either side of the line. From this construction episode comes the famous Euston 'subway', the burrowing pair of lines (up engine and down empty carriage) – a 1 in 50 tunnel with 'backing out' lines from the arrival side across to the western side, to carriage shed and Camden engine shed. There was once again a vast expenditure of cash, particularly in the removal of spoil. A long girder bridge was necessary,

moreover, to carry the four main lines over the 'backing out' lines. As trains now (1993) depart from all platforms, the subway is used not only in emergencies, but at times of congestion to achieve right time departures, releasing platforms to incoming services.

The widening between Euston, Camden and Willesden is labelled 'Sessions 1898 and 1900', the tender going to Joseph F. Firbank for £272,259.19.7d. The firm agreed to "tunnel or subway under Gloucester Road and the bridges under the main line and over the canal, improving approaches and necessary retaining walls on each side between Euston and Camden", to be complete by 1st June 1902 and the remainder of the work, including the carriage shed and roofing and the works at Willesden 'on or before 31st December 1902.' The usual avalanche of detailed costs followed; on July 24th 1901, for instance, the cost of engine power (the LNW hired locos to the contractor) for May and June was (at 1,085 hours, five shillings per hour) put at £271 + £35 for traffic department guards and brakesmen. The quantity of excavation removed now totalled about 17,000 cubic yards, that is 4·3 (old) pence per cubic yard. Slight delay was recorded in late 1901 through difficulty in getting possession of 'a bungalow'. In July 1903 the LNWR agreed to the contractor using his own engine for the haulage of spoil trains. November 1903 saw new workshops at the south end of the new down side carriage shed next to Granby Street. The last of the work took place in 1905/1906; in May 1905 there was still 15,000 cubic yards excavated at Willesden.

Not much more remained now to bring Euston to that marvellously ramshackle back street warren, so despised by the 1960s and so lamented now. The last years of the LNWR saw really only the sort of detail work necessary to 'fine tune' the elements expected of a principal London terminus. *One Who Knew It Well* (he was writing in 1928) describes the years of growing patchwork and clutter thus:

**In about 1912 a commencement was made and gradually carried to completion, of improving generally the accommodation for the convenience of passengers, comprising the following leading features:**

**Extending the covered portion of the cab yard to facilitate the construction of a circulating area (glass roofed) containing an enquiry and booking office, bookstall, and prominent notice boards for the guidance of passengers. Booking offices and refreshment rooms are also conveniently situated on both sides of the station.**

**A handsome dining room was constructed on the west side of the Great**

Hall, whilst on the east side there is a large tea room. There are also waiting rooms, hair dressing rooms, and lavatory accommodation.

Public telephone boxes are to be found in the Great Hall, also seating accommodation is provided for waiting passengers, and interesting models are on view of the Royal Saloon, the 'Rocket', modern locomotives, railway carriages, steamships , etc. On the walls of the Hall are exhibited pictures of the many places of interest situated upon the LMS, which tempt passengers to pay them a visit.

Convenient accommodation is provided for left luggage and for parcels traffic. Milk traffic is dealt with on a separate platform, on the west side, with an approach from Cardington Street. Subways afford access to the booking offices and lifts in connection with the Underground Electric Railways to all parts of London.

Old Euston was never better recalled, to me at least, by the endless corridors of the British Museum – the bits without modern graphics of course. It was the perfect setting for the tense hide and seek scene as John Mills, AWOL to defend his beloved's honour against the wiles of Stewart Granger's spiv, secreted himself in the cafeteria, in the great British film *Waterloo Road*.

By about 1911, when *The Railway and Travel Monthly* ran its feature on the station, Euston had achieved the greatness its London and Birmingham origins had promised years before. "All the world has been there, and will be again" runs the account of 1911 – "it is by no means the largest of railway stations, but there is a distinction even about its name which is eloquent of its importance and fame."

Just so. The description that follows derives largely from James Grants's 1911 account.

"With the slight exception of certain fish, milk and parcels trains" (dealt with separately at bays at platform 10 and 11) Euston was "entirely" a passenger station. About 100 trains a day used Euston in 1911, (rising to 130 in August); three 24 hour pilots fussed about and there were over 30 trains of empty stock to be dealt with. Many of the engines, moreover, (other than those that could be dealt with on the station turntable) had to be worked to or from Camden shed. Six trains with sleeping cars left every night, and 18 equipped with refreshment cars every day. For the purposes of description, Grant declares, Euston could usefully be divided in half, the old and the new...

The old part comprised that area occupied by platforms 1 to 10. 7, 8, 9 and 10 were, strictly speaking for departures, the

*One of the many splendoured glories of Euston, the Great Hall, in May 1953. Its flat panelled ceiling was supposed to the largest of its kind in the world and though it set the pattern for many a noble waiting hall and concourse across the world, its effect upon Euston was something akin to that of an incubus. Sited as it was deep in the middle of the station it forever after determined and distorted subsequent developments.*

others, arrival. D.S. Barrie, in *The Euston to Crewe Companion*, Oakwood Press, 1947, calls No.8 'The York' (York Mails) and 7 'Kensington', for its ancient links to the Kensington via East Croydon service. The work of 1892 had yielded the new part, formed of platforms 11 to 15. No. 2, the box controlling ingress and egress stood plumb in the middle of things, between the two Ampthill Square bridges, Nos 1 and 2. There had been an earlier box, small and cramped, close under the south side of bridge No. 1, at the end of platform 3. This went, it would seem, in the alterations of 1891-2. No.1 box was a peculiar affair; known as 'The Bell House' it was oddly situated, on a gallery over the roadway at platforms 2 and 3. It controlled the working of platforms 1 to 5 and slotted some signals. A number of them were placed on the roof stanchions. No.2 cabin (opened in April 1891) was the principal one, in official notation the 'Station Control

Cabin' and a little beyond stood No. 3, followed by No. 4. The 1890s saw a number of foreign wars which dominated the news sheets of the time – various bits of the Euston layout accordingly had titles relating to world history and the British Empire. Strangely foreign names attached (this was common railway practice – scores of obscure sidings across the country went to their final ends in the 1960s as 'Khartoum', 'Spion Kop' or whatever) themselves and No. 3 box rejoiced in the title of 'Port Arthur'. The other boxes received similar commemorative titles.

The Station Control Cabin was re-equipped around 1910, a new system of locking developed by Mr. A. M. Thompson, the Signal Superintendent at Crewe:

*"...it has superseded the clumsy and antiquated system by which metal weights were attached to the lever rods that range in myriad rows beneath the floor of the cabin. Nearly 300 tons weight of metal has*

*accordingly been removed, and the result has given satisfaction. The system is a safer one, and the levers (of which there are no fewer than 255 in two rows at either side of the long cabin) are easier to pull..."*

The equipment in all the Euston boxes, according to Grant, was of the most modern description – "thoroughly down to date" in an amusing illustration of how the use of phrases can alter over the years. A train indicator in each box showed which platform any incoming train was destined for, and the points worked from boxes 2, 3 and 4 (the latter was the furthest out, close by the subway) were electrically operated. There were also platform indicators, as had been introduced at Kings Cross, informing drivers of incoming trains which platform they would be drawing alongside. Outside the station was a gantry, and beneath each signal against a wooden painted disc, about five feet in diameter a number "was made to appear", indicating the platform.

*Holy of Holies. Inside the Great Hall on 13th December 1954.*

*Faded but animated departure from Euston - 'Problem' or 'Lady of the Lake' class single wheeler No.291 PRINCE OF WALES, scrapped in 1906.*

*Though we lament the passing of Euston and all its works in truth once immediately outside its smoky embrace the surroundings could seem far from salubrious. Part of the clutter fronting Drummond Street, London still in the grip of wartime austerity. June 1945.*

# ROUND AND ABOUT

*This is Eversholt Street and the dire 'Midland Counties Hotel' - for Eversholt Street, read Seymour Street on the map. Now this blackened, boarded up, ramshackle pile of buildings was hardly a fit Gateway To Empire and in truth the ruination and rebuilding of the 1960s, to give us the current windswept Blasted Heath fronting Euston, was really only the culmination of ideas firmly extant as early as the 1930s. In November 1935, after some months of negotiation, the Government had concluded an agreement with all four main railway companies for all manner of reconstruction and improvement, building upon the 1929 Loan Act work already well under way. The LMS share of this largesse included the rebuilding of Euston and the installation of colour light signalling out to Willesden Junction. Plans were advanced by 1937 and indeed an art deco pile was outlined and even recorded for posterity in an 'Artist's Impression'. In terms of the ground covered, this new Euston would be something along the lines of the rebuilding of the 1960s, but look at Euston House, just to the east of Euston now, to get an idea of the style that would have been adopted. 'The Railway Gazette' in September 1938 outlined the new plans without the slightest hint of regret at losing the Arch or the Great Hall, noting that the "scheme involves the demolition of all the buildings between the station and Euston Road in order to enable the platforms to be lengthened and the new station buildings, an hotel, and a block of offices to be erected in a new alignment. Internal accommodation of the station including the concourse, booking office, waiting rooms, refreshment rooms, cloakrooms and other amenities, is planned within the east - west limits of Seymour Street and Melton Street". The whole scheme got as far as Lord Stamp detonating a switch at the Caldon Low quarries in Staffordshire, freeing the first of approximately 100,000 tons of limestone, the hardest (apparently) to be found in Britain. War meant the postponement of all this of course - so, given Depression since 1929, what we now call 'planning blight' since about 1935, war, fire and blitz, poor old Drummond Street and the 'Midland Counties' is probably not in too bad nick after all.*

'The Midland Counties Hotel' and an exit on the east side of the station, 22nd November 1949. This sort of pitiable range of structures represents the high water mark of the 1870s enlargement episode. The whole of the works came into use in 1874 - the widening of the station on the eastern, Seymour Street side provided additional lines and platforms, a large extension of the roofing, the making of a new approach from the Euston Road by cutting through the gardens in Euston Square and many other improvements which added up to nearly three extra acres. 'Virol', a sweet malty stuff, was made in a factory out at Alperton. It seems no railway picture before about 1958 is complete without an advert for it.

22nd November 1949. This is Drummond Street, looking towards Eversholt Street, the dear old 'Midland Counties' is on the corner there and if anything this bit of street was even more run down, dilapidated, decayed and derelict - a lethargy gripped the area prior to 'comprehensive redevelopment' (a post-War phrase to chill us) and uncertainty haunted the surroundings of the station really all through the 1950s.

*More shadowy corners at Euston, June 1945.*

*Whatever the world's best wave was, the perm was certainly an institution, only too familiar from mothers and sisters. Eugene (permanently yours) did little to liven the dullness at Euston, but it was a decent enough start. June 1945.*

*New cinema like "Train Arrival Bureau", 1st June 1953 - for inside, see later. Beyond is the vast monolith of Euston House. The new Euston of Lord Stamp would have looked something like this and the jumbled free-for-all would have been transformed, more thoroughly maybe than the subsequent 1960s works.*

*Lord Stamp's corporate giantism, 24th September 1953. The Truman's pub (still there as far as I recall - the Engine Shed Society once met there) is a bit reminiscent of the Laings suburban showhouse erected in the shadow of Kings Cross. See the first Irwell 'Great British Station' - Kings Cross.*

18

*Your vehicle awaits. Daimler, 21st April 1955.*

**Euston was blackened under the fume and smoke of the greatest Industrial Revolution wrought in this world. In a good old London description is was, truly, as "black as Newgate's* knocker". Some at least of the lovely stonework is emerging during cleaning work here, 24th May 1955. *The infamous prison, pronounced Noogit's.**

*Drummond Street looking more or less west and the brooding arch, June 1945. Euston, as James Scott rightly claimed, was "chaste and classic in its exterior and main approach. In coming to its Doric arch and passing between the colonnades of it into the main square, one could imagine one's self entering the quadrangle of an old university".*

*Taxis lined up around the network of roads off Ampthill Square; these thirty or so are on what would be Ampthill Square No.1 on the plan. Barnaby Street lies ahead, Euston station underneath to the right, out of sight. Photograph by arrangement John Tatchell.*

*Eastern end of Drummond Street, June 1945, with two anonymous lodges; there were two each side - the opposite, western-most one, has been demolished to make way for offices.*

*More cleaning at Euston, 21st April 1955. How might these cluttered but grand buildings fully restored have been cherished, had this little neighbourhood been preserved. A new Covent Garden, maybe...*

Much of the buildings in and around Euston had an almost cyclopian look, some inter-connected system of vaulted tombs maybe. The new brickwork, so sharply at odds with the stone backdrop, would be anti-blast screens. Photograph dated June 1945. These are the offices fronting Drummond Street, immediately to the west of the arch.

Every citizen should know about VD! The exigency of war had rapidly allowed minor prudery to be dispensed with and for Britain alone (among the western combatants at least) totally mobilised in its population, such niceties were an early and inevitable casualty. Again perfect image of end of war Britain - June 1945.

Euston, low down below street level, had insinuated itself into this little bit of north London. This made it, historically, difficult to photograph and there are very few of the stirring images we get from say Kings Cross, St. Pancras, Waterloo and the rest. Its patchwork nature is quite evident and the sheer extent of the site has rarely been so well represented. Far off lies Lord Stamp's Euston House and the train below bears the boards "London Euston - Blackpool Central". The lorry is parked in Ampthill Square, the other Ampthill Square, No. 1 on the map, lying beyond with Barnaby Street disappearing into the distance. Date is 21st June 1951, with resignalling under way; the far bridge (see later in the book) is boarded off at its end, ready for removal. The No.2 box, also to be removed, lies centre left - again see later in the book.

There was something dignified and sedate about Euston which was somehow denied the other main termini, despite the dilapidated surroundings. Moreover there seems to have been a never-ending series of what could almost be described as antechambers before passengers found themselves actually out in the dazzling daylight of London proper. As a child in the 'fifties on an early trip out unaccompanied (parents blithely under the impression we were trainspotting a hundred yards from home in north London) I found it an alarmingly confusing place. Above, 27th March 1959, typifies the hurried bustle you took your life in your hands with the cabs whizzing about - and below (June 1945) more sombre times. 'RTO' shot through with an arrow denoted 'Railway Transport Office' - essential for the hordes of soldiers on the move.

*Decoration to one of the preserved little lodges - more or less all that remains, perched oddly close by the Euston Road. These were the two lodges inscribed with a (often highly optimistic) litany of destinations which the prospective traveller could reach from Euston. Much of it sailed close to the wind of whatever passed for the Trades Description Act. The same group could be found above the Board office door in the Great Hall - see earlier picture.*

*The Great Hall on 21st April 1953. The statue is of George Stephenson (Robert was out the front in the open). It could still be described with great pride in 1911 "it is spacious, well lit and of imposing height. A gallery with ornamental railing is carried around the hall thus forming a pleasing break in the massiveness of the walls. In the centre of the hall stands an admirable statue of George Stephenson and the floor is occupied by rows of seats for waiting passengers, train indicators, models of the steamers running from Holyhead to Ireland, afternoon tearooms, weighing and chocolate machines and all the usual equipment of a station waiting hall. From one end of the hall broad flights of steps lead up to the extensive Offices of the Company which range inwards to a bewildering extent on either side."*

*Corridor of power.*

There is a famous description of Euston in a series "The Fascination of Railway Stations" in a long lamented magazine, 'The Railway and Travel Monthly'. One line runs amusingly, "no-one visits railway stations to study architecture!" and indeed throughout much of the Euston warren fine architecture would be the last thing to occur to anybody. Entering the courtyard behind the arch the passenger was at once "on the fringe of the station's stir". The absence of trolleys is said to be one great boon of the new great glass hall of the modern Euston, and one can see why...

Presumably simple tonic won out over votrix long ago and it probably wouldn't have been standard fare in the Midland Counties Hotel... 1st June 1953.

End of war view, June 1945 - "most of the glass covering of the cavernous shadowy train sheds was destroyed in the Battle of Britain, leaving platforms open to the sky. Women were always many at Euston. Pink faced, trim Wrens bound for naval stations on windy, rain swept coasts of western and northern Scotland; American WACs and nurses, ATS girls going to new stations or back to work from holiday, like the men heavily encumbered with equipment and girls with similar uniforms, many wearing the sign of European Allied Nations on their shoulders and CWACs from Manitoba, Saskatchewan, Alberta, Quebec and all the provinces of Canada, WAAFs in RAF blue and Land Girls in trim hats, sweaters and riding pants". And there were of course Yanks, as 'A US Officer' (quoted above and in the text) was happy to recall - "one caught all the accents of Boston, Bangor, New Orleans, Denver, 'Frisco. On their shoulders they wore the badges of half a hundred divisions and everywhere many from the AAF. Some were still training, others had been in Africa, Sicily, Salerno, Casino; others had made the assault on the Omaha or Utah beaches, back now to a land they were surprised to find they love so much. Thousands had been quartered in small villages where, like animals in a zoo, they had first watched local people, while farmers and tradesmen had scrutinised them with mutual curiosity until at length they became acquainted. Now their tongues were used to English words and phrases. In some deep sense they felt at home."

*Holidays already in the air, June 1945.*

*Military presence in June 1945.*

*Euston on 22nd November 1949, all cobbles and glass.*

One of the more bizarre peculiarities of Euston station (which in general seemed to owe very little to conventional ideas of form and arrangement) was the old No.1 box hoisted above the cab road between platforms 2 and 3. It dated from the 1870s and remained in use for the workings of platforms 1 to 5. Communication between it and No.2 box was a by ringing code system (hence its name, the 'bell' box) and describers. These two pictures show it on 1st October 1952, just as it was being taken out of use upon the resignalling of that year - see later.

*Above and below. Cabs cabs cabs, if anything Euston had cabs. This is the roof over the roadway between Nos 2 and 3 platforms, the same roadway straddled by the peculiar No.1, or 'bell' box (it 'belled' trains in). Date is 22nd February 1956.*

# WAR AND PEACE

*The time of the coat over the arm - characteristic Euston bustle, 14th July 1953, viewed, it would seem, from the 'bell' box. What sort of pell mell confusion this was in wartime can only be guessed at. Our anonymous US officer remembered Euston for its black sepulchral qualities "Dear God, what joys and sorrows Euston station holds in its keeping! Dirty black and shabby in its externals but like a faithful workman doing a necessary job he had a quality of honesty which spoke louder than surface beauty."*

The LMS renovated the Great Hall in 1927 but the station very largely mouldered as bits were patched up or added or painted. In July 1929 the LMS came up with four separate schemes to combine Euston with St. Pancras, which were so extraordinary that it will serve well to briefly detail them here:

**1. New through station ½ mile north of the Euston Road.**
**2. New terminus fronting Euston Road, midway between Euston and St. Pancras.**
**3. New terminus fronting Euston Road, but further to the west, between Hampstead Road and Albany Street.**
**4. Remodelling and enlargement of Euston, bringing frontage onto Euston Road.**

Schemes 2, 3 and 4 envisaged a double track tunnel for Midland line trains, between Finchley and Chalk Farm. These ideas seem bizarre enough now but their boldness alone must have much to commend them. When we look at what we eventually did to Euston, no past proposals deserve our scorn. The Great Slump would have scuppered the 1929 ideas, even if they were wholly serious, but this was just one more scrape with redevelopment, so far as Euston was concerned. The Boer War had stopped one wholesale proposal, the Great War a second, and World War Two yet a third.

The Second World War left Euston in a sort of panting exhaustion. It had survived the conflict much as any big British station, from Lancashire to London – bashed about with a few nights of bloody horror much outnumbered by an endless chaos of overcrowding, blackout and delay somewhere else 'up the line'. The *London Midland Magazine* published a moving article (together with a photograph of the damage in October 1940, when a bomb landed between platforms 2 and 3) in 1952, attri-buted simply to 'A U.S. Officer' and one or two extracts recall those times.

...its bookstalls were heavily patronised. There were good volumes there for the traveller, on many subjects; never enough papers to go around – but then, people would share their reading. And there was a little sweet shop, generally with barren shelves. When chocolate was in, queues formed up quickly from nowhere. Flowers shone in bright colours from a stall always with women and children in front of it – those who are fed by beauty. Men would come out holding a few bright blooms for home, or sweetheart, or hospital. Once I went with a Canadian who purchased a single rose. He carried it in his hand all the way to Carlisle. It spoke to him of something, or someone I did not know. We never mentioned it as, a hundred times in the long night, he held it to his face.

Nights when raids were on, people walked deliberately with exaggerated slowness, just to convince their scared souls they were not afraid. With tense steps, under dimmed blue lights, they sought out taxis or red concealed signs of the Underground.

Sometimes bombs fell close, rattling down glass like the tinkling of ice, and on a few nights they were on their target. Emergency crews worked round the clock – soon trains were running again....

....At all hours passengers sorted themselves out in one of the earth's most populous cities, for ports and camps of the South, and West, and North. But morning arrivals of military trains and evening ones for the North stirred me most deeply.

Generally at night there were three trains for the North, one or two requisitioned by the Air Ministry, the Admiralty, or the War Office. These were high priority affairs and only those with special reasons might ride.

Passengers arrived for hours before departure time, on foot, by Underground, in taxi, and truck loads of service people laden like camels, with duffle* bags, knapsacks, rifles, tommy guns, all sorts of equipment. Long queues formed before gates. When they were opened tickets were examined, and once beyond the barrier there was a rush for seats. When one had found a seat or a place to stand there was time to catch breath and to see on platforms as vivid a vignette of War behind battle fronts as was possible to behold in any moment of the life of a soldier, sailor or airman....

....As time crept on eyes would search the clock. Railway clocks are some way different from all other clocks. They have a certain finality, and inexorable quality. No one questions them. They move, you obey. Baggage cleared away, more and more talked through windows, doors banged with a dreadful conclusiveness. Some who had come to say goodbye, feeling it would ease the burden, would depart, but others stayed, silently holding a hand outstretched from a carriage window or door, saying without speech what tongues could not utter. A sharp whistle, kisses, goodbyes.

Women porters would pick up odd pieces of lost luggage. The long train would gather speed, night after night, year after year the same, always new, always poignant....

....Dear God, what joys and sorrows Euston station holds in its keeping! Dirty and black and shabby in its externals, but, like a faithful workman doing a necessary job, it had a quality of honesty which spoke louder than surface beauty.

Crowding and confusion reigned at Euston through the War, as at all other major stations. Bombing at Kilburn for instance would cut off the terminus completely, passengers going to Willesden Junction by

*Remember the narrator is American; British servicemen carried kit...

electric train to catch a steam train there. Passengers for Manchester, say, or Birmingham, would be advised to go to St Pancras or Paddington, unthinkable advice in earlier times. High explosive bombs blocked LMS lines as late as February 1944, at Canonbury and West Hampstead; there were no less than 83 incidents on the LMS from 1st January to 14th June that year, and on 22 of these occasions track was blocked. Flying bombs were flung in the fray in June and fell in England even until 31st August, with 26th August the only day spared. 128 'Doodlebugs' fell on the LMS, the debris from one one blocking the electric lines at Wembley on 4th July. Long range rockets, V2s, came in September and in November the Germans claimed to have demolished Euston station "but fortunately this claim, like many others they made, was untrue and the Company were left to solve the problem of designing a modern station without the assistance of German science." (*LMS War Report* – in typically British fashion labelled *Most Secret,* 1944).

Men were expected to reach the depots, camps and regiments on time, and offices existed at places like Euston where special 'chits' could be signed, certifying that the delay was due to legitimate, railway operating reasons, or to enemy action. The U.S Officer's poignant piece on Euston was felt by the editor of *London Midland Magazine,* plainly, to overstate somewhat the

*Euston June 1945.*

gloomy decrepitude and war weariness of the place: *Should the writer revisit Euston a footnote runs, he will find that whilst retaining all its characteristics, it is now a lot brighter than during the War.*

Already, in the autumn of 1944, the War in Europe set for Victory, thought began to turn to the revivification of Euston and a detailed appraisal was made of the arrangements, to show up, as much as anything, its drawbacks.

From an operating point of view the station by 1944 (and the following detail applies for really most of the LMS proprietorship of the station – and LNW days after about 1905, of course) comprised twenty six lines of varying lengths, fifteen of them platform lines, and the remainder providing stabling accommodation. There were, it will be seen, some altogether prominent disabilities, surprising in the nation's foremost station, which frequently required to be surmounted. Summarised, the fifteen platforms were as follows:-

| Platform No. | Length* | Number of Coaches** |
|---|---|---|
| 1. Arrival | 1,022 | 15 |
| 2. Arrival | 1,028½ | 15 |
| 3. Arrival | 867 | 11 |
| 4. Arr. & Dep. – Local Steam+Electric | 623 | 10 Down Steam, 9 Up Steam, 9 Electric |
| 5. Arr. & Dep. – Local Steam+Electric and Horse Landing | 577½† | 9 Down Steam, 8 Up Steam, 9 Electric |
| 6. Departure | 862½ | 14 Down, 13 Up |
| 7. Departure – Local Steam, Arr. & Dep. – Electric | 427¾ | 7 Steam, 6 Electric |
| 8. Departure | 385¾ | 6 Down |
| 9. Departure | 624½ | 10 |
| 10. Departure – Parcels and Newspapers | 676½ | 10 |
| 11. Departure (dock) – Parcels, Newspapers etc. | 497½ | 8 |
| 12. Departure | 926 | 15 |
| 13. Departure | 1,068 | 17 |
| 14. Departure | 996¾ | 16 |
| 15. Departure | 930⅓ | 15 |

*from buffer face level to top of ramp (in feet).
**=accommodation for coaches of 60ft. 8in. overall length + engine.
†distance from top of ramp to position opposite buffer face level on No. 4 platform. Total length of platform 839¾ ft.

*Dull and Drear 1. June 1945; this would be somewhere over on the west side - an old Green Line 'T' is on ambulance service.*

*Dull and Drear 2. Soldiers amid the clutter, over on the west side by the look of things, June 1945 - kit bags, wicker work, ladders, signs, bicycles, all the flotsam and jetsam of a big complex station.*

*Dull and Drear 3. And uninviting to boot. A highly atmospheric view in June 1945, the route down to the Underground more reminiscent of some terrible dungeon of the Gestapo than the London & Birmingham's pride and joy.*

*There was always another corner to round at Euston - this is the distinctive little area at the ends of Platforms 13, 14 and 15, June 1945.*

*Ticket collection for Platforms 12, 13 etc. June 1945.*

*A further discrete little piece of Euston, June 1945. On the trolley is laundry from one of the myriad sleepers, ready to take to the big LMS Laundry, out by the West London line at Willesden Junction.*

*Booking Hall area, June 1945 again uniforms predominate.*

Long suspecting that the laws of economics are anything but, Irwell Press would be quite happy to see a new economic indicator - the style and amount of advertising. It would probably be as sensitive as any. Life was picking up in 1950s Britain - witness above (23rd June 1950) and below (22nd February 1956) labelled "Departure Side Improvements". The 'Railbar', grim and boarded up above, is brewing brightly with steaming tea below and although it is 1956, there is still the omnipresent army greatcoat.

## No. 1 Platform

A train arriving with one engine and seventeen coaches fouled the connection from the Up Fast Line, into the other arrival platforms. It also prevented the disposal engine coming to the rear of the train via Up Engine Line No. 2. It therefore had to travel to Camden No. 1 Box, cross all lines there, and work over the Up Fast Line on to its train. In addition, the two rear vehicles, if they were loaded brakes, had to be shunted off the train and placed in another platform for the luggage to be unloaded.

A train arriving on No. 1 which exceeded one engine and thirteen coaches had, when emptied, to run out via the Down Empty Carriage Line – if the coaches required to be stabled at Willesden. It was not possible to despatch a train of this length via the Down Fast or Down Slow Lines; after travelling via the Down Empty Carriage Line the empty coaches had to be crossed at Camden No. 1 – over the Down Fast Line to get to the Down Slow Line. A train over the Down Empty Carriage Line reacted upon the disposal of trains running from other platforms to the down side carriage shed by this route which, in turn, could retard the marshalling of down trains at the Shed.

## No. 2 Platform

The problems multiplied across the station as longer trains filled the various platforms; as options closed down the defects became more ever more manifest. How they coped in the War is anyone's guess – trains, as on the LNER into Kings Cross, must have divided and all manner of impromptu signalling reverted to. Arriving at No. 2 platform a train exceeding one engine and thirteen coaches prevented a train ready to leave No. 1 platform for Willesden getting access to either the Fast or Slow lines; consequently it would either have to be held until No. 2 platform was cleared, or despatched via the Down Empty Carriage Line and crossed at Camden, as referred to above.

If a train arrived at No. 2 with more than fifteen vehicles and one engine, the empty coaches could not be worked to Willesden via the Down Fast Line, but of necessity went via the Down Slow Line or via the Down Empty Carriage Line. The TPO left from No.2, just about the only 'proper' departure this side.

At the north end, owing to the taxi overbridge, No. 2 platform was very narrow and caused congestion with luggage parcels, mails and so on. "preventing the expeditious unloading of vans." The Up postal prior to the Second War, generally fifteen vehicles, was due to arrive Euston at 3.55 am, and to meet Post Office requirements, had to be dealt with in this platform. In consequence of the narrow space available, the train had to be split and the five rear vehicles shunted in to No. 3 platform. This movement and occupation of two arrival platforms with one train was frequently the cause of delay.

## No. 3 Platform

This was a difficult platform to work; it would only accommodate one engine and eleven vehicles inside 'clear of bar'† and when, as frequently happened, a train of fifteen vehicles and one engine had to be accommodated, the rear portion stood foul, preventing empty coaches leaving either No. 1 or No. 2 platforms over the Fast Line to Willesden. It prevented an empty coach train leaving No. 1 platform for Willesden via the Slow Line and denied passage to a train off the Up Slow Line, running in to No. 1 platform.

An engine with more than eleven vehicles standing at No. 3 would not allow a train to be brought in to Nos. 4 and 5 platforms over the Up Slow Line; such a train would necessarily be crossed to the Down Slow Line via No. 2 Box, thus in turn preventing a train leaving Nos. 5, 6, 7, 8 or 9 platforms via the Down Slow Line. This, of course, reacted on shunting movements to and from these platforms.

## No. 4 Platform

There is a sense of mounting complication in this account of the Euston platforms (the official LMS Review from which it is

†*Fouling, or detector bar, just inside the running rail and depressed by flanges of any vehicle standing there. No fouling movements could then be made. Vital when out of sight of signalman – superseded by track circuits.*

***Leaky roof, 23rd June 1950.***

culled was surely laying the baseline for post War rebuilding) though No. 4 was straightforward enough, being used for local steam and electric trains.

### No. 5 Platform

Devoted to local steam and electric services, whilst at the south end serving as a horse landing. As a war time measure the south end was used for loading forwarded parcels post traffic and vans were in position practically throughout the day.

### No. 6 Platform

No. 6 was a departure platform, though it had frequently to be turned over to incoming trains. The lack of a roadway for taxis or other vehicles proved a liability, and when a train had to be run in to this platform, considerable inconvenience ensued for passengers.

Fifteen vehicles in here with an engine fouled No. 5 platform completely and blocked departures from Nos. 7, 8 and 9 platforms via the east side of No. 2 Box, otherwise the proper route to avoid delaying shunting operations on the west side of the station. No.6 seems to have been the usual platform for the complete Royal Train.

### No. 7 Platform

Used for arrival and departure of local steam and electric trains, as well as Up parcels.

### No. 8 Platform

Served for Down local steam trains, and forwarded parcels and parcels post traffic.

### No. 9 Platform

No. 9 was used for main line and local steam services, also for parcels trains, and occasionally for arrivals.

### No. 10 Platform

For forwarded parcels and newspaper traffic, but if not occupied by such traffic, it could serve for Down passenger workings.

### No. 11 Platform (Dock)

Forwarded and received parcels post, letter mails, newspapers etc. and similar traffic in 'through loads'.

### Nos. 12 and 13 Platforms

A train of seventeen vehicles with engines front and rear standing at No. 13 platform prevented a train being set or despatched Fast Line from No. 12 platform. The straggling narrowness of these platforms at the north end was always a disadvantage.

### Nos. 14 and 15 Platforms

The author of the LMS Investigation was unimpressed by the east side altogether: "the narrowness of these platforms

also, and the approach to them, are a continual source of trouble." Particular difficulty was experienced in getting luggage and parcels to the front of the trains to load them into the proper vans, such was the congestion as the platforms attenuated to their extremities.

In an ancient site such as Euston, it was not surprising that sidings abounded – between 5 and 6 platform lines was 'the Horse Box Line' for instance, which could accommodate no less than 13 vehicles assuming a length of 60ft. 8in.). The 'Irish Mail Line' lay at the west side of No. 7 platform and the '2nd Line' (4 vehicles moved by standard 3F tank – other engines prohibited) on the east side of No. 8 platform. Between these two were 'No. 8 Road' and 'No. 5 Road' both used for wagons only and known as 'The Field'.

'The Pilot Siding' and 'The Carriage Dock', holding a single bogie vehicle and a six wheel vehicle each, stood at the north end of platforms 10 and 11 and 'The Pit Road', accommodating six 60ft. 8in. vehicles, lay between platforms 11 and 12. 'No. 2 Road' for 16 vehicles, stood between 13 and 14 and 'No. 18 Road' (for 13 vehicles) lay at the west side of No. 15 platform. The very westernmost road, to the west of No. 18 Road, was 'The Loco Road', holding seven vehicles clear of the ashpit. Beside this variously convenient stabling, there was further accommodation at the carriage sheds (which had come about in the construction episode concluded around 1905):

### Up Carriage Shed

Situated approximately ½ mile north of the station on the Up side of the line. It was used for the stabling of local steam and electric trains; of its five roads Nos. 1 and 2 held seven electric or steam vehicles, Nos. 2 and 4 seven electric or eight steam vehicles and No. 5 road, the longest, fourteen electric or fifteen steam vehicles. It was a 'dead end' shed (stop blocks at the north end) with connection to and from platforms 1 to 9, via 'The Independent Line.'

### Down Carriage Shed

The down shed, which stabled main line express train stock, lay just under ½ mile north of the station on the down side of the line. The early morning group of trains to the north (except Scotland) and the Up evening group of such trains were dealt with here instead of at Willesden, one of the reasons being to avoid line occupation between Euston and Willesden during the morning and evening group of main line and residential trains. Its accommodation was measured once again in 60ft. 8in. vehicles; No. 1 road held thirteen, Nos. 2 and 3 a dozen each, Nos. 4 and 5 held ten, No. 6 took eleven and No. 7 took nine. Roads No. 8 and 9 held eight vehicles each, No. 10 held sixteen and No. 11 berthed only four coaches. The Down Carriage Shed was again a 'dead end' shed (stop blocks at the south end in this instance) with connection from any platforms via the 'Backing Out Roads' or from plat-

*Framed view into the lengthy western departure platforms, 12 to 15, 2nd June 1955. This was the side brought into use in the early 1890s together with separate booking office and cab entrance into Drummond Street. It's been said before - it certainly was a station within a station, leading to endless confusion. This was the side taken over to Cardington Street which involved the exhumation of corpses and their interment in St. Pancras Cemetery, Finchley, one of the more bizarre expenditures in the LNWR ledger books.*

*At last we get to trains. Willesden 2-6-4T No.42367, having brought in a train to Platform 14, 6th April, 1962.*

*June 1945 and the old passimeter booking office/barrier to the dc Platforms 4 and 5. Oerlikon electric train just visible to the left. The service, it is interesting to note, was half hourly outside the peak - today it is three an hour.*

*Euston 22nd November 1949. The old destination board holds some gems - 'MORCAMBE (PROM)' for instance.*

forms 1 to 9 via the Down and Up Empty Carriage Lines. There was also connection to any platform via the Backing Out roads or Up Engine Line No. 1.

An empty Down train of not more than fourteen 60ft. 8in. vehicles together with standard shunting 3F tank could be drawn out of the shed and propelled to the platforms via the Backing Out roads, or left in one of these roads. A train of greater length however, had to be drawn out on to the Down Empty Carriage Line before being set back to the Backing Out roads. This prevented an engine from Camden shed or a train of empty coaches from Willesden to Euston, on the Up Empty Carriage Line and Up Engine Line No. 1, running into the platforms.

### Backing Out Roads

Four roads were provided between the main line and the Down Carriage Shed and connection to and from any platform was possible. Labelled Nos. 1, 2, 3 and 4 (accommodating 12, 12, 13 and 15 60ft. 8in. vehicles respectively) they served principally for completed empty trains awaiting platform acceptance. Occasionally an empty train from the arrival platforms

might be disposed via these roads, when the Down Empty Carriage Line was full. No. 4 was primarily a running round road and was not used for holding purposes.

### Coal Stage Siding

Held one bogie and one 6-wheeled vehicle. Situated at the station end of the Backing Out Roads, connection was made from Nos. 4 and 3 Backing Out roads.

### General

Between Camden No. 1 Box and Euston there were four main lines: Up Fast (East Side); Up Slow (electrified); Down Slow (electrified); Down Fast. The Up lines – Fast and Slow – had connections to platforms Nos. 1 to 9 inclusive, for steam trains. Electric trains could only use Platforms Nos. 4, 5 and 7 and connection was off the Up Slow.

Both Fast and Slow Down had connections from platforms Nos. 1 to 12 inclusive for steam trains, but from Platforms Nos.

13, 14 and 15 trains could only leave via the Fast line. Electric sets from platforms 4, 5 and 7 left on the Slow.

### Up Empty Carriage Line

The Up Empty Carriage served for empties from Willesden to Euston – the connection was from the Up Slow Main at Camden No. 2 Box. It burrowed underneath the main lines opposite Camden shed and emerged on the Down side between Camden No. 1 and Euston No. 4 boxes; thence it converged with the Up Engine line No. 1 into the station. Empty coaches from Willesden could also travel over the Up Slow Main to Euston No. 4, crossing at that point to Engine Line No. 1. This operation prevented trains leaving Euston by the Main lines. This borrowing single track was the 'rat 'ole' of evil repute and a crew would go to great lengths to ensure a clear trip through – stalling could be positively dangerous in its fume-laden, close confines. It was the scene of at least

one 'rescue', in late BR days, when a train of empty stock from Willesden with a Fowler 2-6-2T stalled in 'the 'ole'. Fortunately one of the 'twins', 10000 or 10001, was available and a loco inspector (who was later commended) took the diesel in, using the nose doors to gain access and couple up, drawing the train out to the living world.

### Up Engine Line No. 1

It ran from Camden engine shed, to converge with the Up Empty Carriage line between Camden No. 1 and Euston No. 4 boxes, and thence close into the terminus, connecting to all platforms. The converging of the Up Engine line and the Up Empty Carriage between Camden No. 1 and Euston No. 4 Boxes entailed careful regulation if delay in platforming stock and engines for Down trains was to be avoided, not to mention the running of engines to Engine Line No. 2.

### Water etc.

Water for locomotives could be taken at Euston on platforms 3, 4, 5, 6, 7 and 10, on the Horse Box Line, the Pilot Siding and Loco Road. A 60ft. turntable (dating from the early 1930s, it would seem) was set on the extreme west side of the station, serving for both locomotive and carriage purposes. There were three short roads off the turntable for Outdoor Machinery Department wagons and for coke for the stationary steam heating boilers.

*Above - Platforms 12 and 13, part of the west side departures, 23rd June 1950. Below - looking for all the world like a Forces cinema, set up behind the lines somewhere, was an area where train information was projected onto screens, mesmerized passengers plotting the disasters awaiting them. Here it is newly installed, 1st June 1953.*

*Above - Euston with one of the pride and joys of Watford - BR Standard 4MT tank No.80068 on 19th May 1957. Platforms 4 and 5 had dc - note the rails ending short on 5 - though a mix of steam and electric turned up during the peak. Photograph H.C. Casserley. Below - diesels take over amid the bustle and the morning crush, 1962.*

*Princes Royal No. 46204 PRINCESS LOUISE alongside that lovely classic, curving, Platform No.2. A beautiful place where light poured in from the right and the station shrank into darkness over line upon line to the left. All principal arrivals were on this side and about the only train to depart from here, unless some tremendous emergency had broken out, was the Postal. 14th July 1953.*

*Disembodied clientele on 29th April 1954. Art deco, steel and glass booths (the 'Empire Fruit Stall' no less!) creeping in. There are advertising exhibits in the glass cases; Wymans became Menzies and where now is the ghostly little girl?*

*This was 'fifties Britain. From days of dearth after the War the country was rising fast, though in many ways it was still determinedly down at heel and still fairly regimented. Notices and arrows ensure a perfectly ordered (what else?) British queue. 16th August 1958.*

*Sundries loading at Euston, a fine old range from the days when the railways took the lot - wicker baskets and dented tins, sacks, nameless rod like implements and even half a dozen galvanised pails. And only three men to see them off.*

*The Euston rush again, as good a social indicator as might be found anywhere - all suits and cases, the general decline of the hat, pretty frocks and a Crewe North Royal Scot, 46151 THE ROYAL HORSE GUARDSMAN in Platform 1. 8th August 1953.*

*46204 again on 14th July 1953, splendidly cut in half by light and shade.*

*Wrought iron colonnade and famous curving cab rank between 2 and 3. An entrance to the Northern Line lurks beyond in the iron work - the Underground at Euston was notable for a couple of appalling, clanging, banging, lurching lifts, manned by a crusty individual whose purpose in life was to slam the gates just before the noses of panting passengers.*

*Euston corner - end of Platform 5 road.*

*Euston, 27th November 1951 and the newly ballasted three roads between 13 and 14. A high, precarious footbridge crossed the departure side, though I have not been able to determine its precise purpose.*

*Doom is nigh. Though the operation was done with great skill and was a miracle of planning acumen, the heart was nevertheless torn out of Euston. This is the middle part, looking for all the world like the shrivelled iron work left after an air raid; nearest Platform is No.4, Platform 3 is gone, with far platform (2 or 1?) still in use. 12th April 1963, Photograph Alec Swain.*

Spectacular departure of 46150 THE LIFE GUARDSMAN with The Irish Mail on 17th July 1954, illustrating the difficulties of obtaining stirring spectacles on film at Euston, though removal of the bridge did improve matters. There was no fine backdrop as at Kings Cross, with sunlight playing into open platforms. Euston was often a smoke wreathed place to boot, and opportunities for good photography were accordingly restricted. Not this time though.

# CHAPTER FOUR

# TRAINS TO REMEMBER

*Glorious light and shade at Euston, inevitably punctuated by randomly arranged trolleys, barrows, packets, parcels and bundles and - The Royal Scot awaiting departure for Glasgow, 31st July 1955. Scene is probably between Platforms 13 and 14. As the 'fifties wore on Euston reached again the end of an old familiar cycle - enlargement and extension of services beyond the confines of the track and platforms, rather after the fashion of an animal which needs to periodically burst its shell and grow a new one. There were over 400 trains in and out every 24 hours with 50,000 long distance and 20,000 suburban passengers on a normal summers day around this time, BR staff at Euston amounting to an astonishing 1,055 by 1957. In addition to The Royal Scot and perhaps the other great stalwart, The Irish Mail, both of which we have now seen, by the summer of 1957 the following named trains graced Euston; The Red Rose and The Merseyside Express for Liverpool; The Midday Scot for Glasgow; The Shamrock for Liverpool/Ireland; The Mancunian, The Comet and The Lancastrian for Manchester; The Ulster Express - Heysham for Belfast; The Lakes Express for Windermere - Workington; The Welshman for Portmadoc and other North Wales resorts; The Midlander for Birmingham; The Manxman for Liverpool (for Isle of Man); The Northern Irishman (Stranraer for Larne and Belfast); The Caledonian for Glasgow and The Royal Highlander for Inverness.*

*People and Trains 1. Sweet sorrow of parting for the Welshman on 14th July 1953. Britain is still a country where military uniform is familiar and Euston is obviously still a heavily portered station, its workings still firmly in the traditional way of things. Military figure is a Warrant Officer in The Royal Signals. And who is the group eyeing him? One is in particularly strange garb - eastern European refugees?*

*People and Trains 2. The Royal Scot in the unaccustomed charge of a diesel (one of the Southern 1Co-Co1 locos) on 16th August 1958. Looks to be Platform 3.*

*People and Trains 3. 14th July 1953, and an arrival on No.2 behind a Princess.*

*People and Trains 4. No date for this one but a timeless enough scene. An evocative picture which somehow captures the way railways were - more at the heart of peoples' lives in that far off vanished aeon of the 1950s.*

*The great glory of Euston, during a long period of steam, was of course the Pacifics, and few people caught them to better effect then Peter Groom. This is The Midday Scot leaving Euston on 21st of May 1956 behind DUCHESS OF SUTHERLAND, fair fit to burst with steam and power. Photograph Peter Groom.*

*Inaugural run of the Coronation Scot, behind 6220 CORONATION - 5th July 1937.*

*Attentive audience for a 1930s departure of The Coronation Scot, leaving Euston behind streamlined 6223 PRINCESS ALICE.*

*Euston in the 1930s once more. Compounds were long regarded as something of a rarity at Euston though 1161, based in Manchester, is only incidental to C.R.L. Coles experiments with lighting. By the 1950s these 4-4-0s had certainly become scarce in London on the LNW and were more or less unknown by 1956. It was thus startling in 1958 when one of Rugby's, more accustomed to pottering about to Peterborough, turned up on a Rugby - Euston diagram. Astonishingly, another Compound appeared the next afternoon and a similar sequence took place the following year. Photograph C.R.L. Coles.*

*6211 QUEEN MAUD with The Midday Scot, an extreme platform end view which proves that no corner of Euston was without its trolley - 'The Corridor' (an old LNW term, from the days when such stock was new and marvellous) was bereft of headboard at this time.*

*9th September 1931 and a Claughton 4-6-0, 5975 TALISMAN. Photograph H.C. Casserley.*

*Claughton again, 6004 at Euston on 30th July 1939. This was the only one to survive (by some years; the last but one going in 1941) till nationalisation, though the alloted 46004 was never carried. Photograph H.C. Casserley.*

*Truly a rarity, Hughes L&Y type 4-6-0 No. 10471, backing out of the station after bringing a childrens excursion from Blackpool in 1934. Photograph C.R.L. Coles.*

It is probably fairly clear from these photographs so far that Euston could at times own a pervading gloomy air. It could also be surprisingly empty at odd periods during the day and I well remember my first visit in the 1950s, where the place seemed almost dead compared to the mad tumult of Kings Cross and Paddington, taken in on the same day. After a prolonged wait we were forced to go on the tramp to Camden for our first Pacifics. Euston really came blazingly to life every night, especially Saturday with the newspaper traffic. 3F tanks (7467 is on Platform 3) were just about the only non-passenger type at Camden shed and were frequently put on to pilot work. 30th July 1939. Photograph H.C. Casserley.

Left. 2-6-4 tank No.2444 making a bold show of things, 11th November 1938. Photograph H. C. Casserley.

Pair of Royal Scots at 1 and 2. A classically stirring combination, 46153 THE ROYAL DRAGOON from Manchester and a homegrown London engine 46139 THE WELCH REGIMENT. Photograph C.R.L. Coles.

*Further brace of Scots, 46155 THE LANCER (ex-GW Syphon behind?) and 46116 IRISH GUARDSMAN.*

*Princess Royal Pacific 46207 PRINCESS ARTHUR OF CONNAUGHT on "The Corridor", above - quiescent (well relatively) before a blasting exit (below) on 31st August 1961. This was the last time a "Royal" was diagrammed to work this train it is thought - though of course steam continued frequent substitutions for diesels in the troubled 1960s when English Electric Type 4s fitfully took over the West Coast duties. In the 1950s at least Pacifics were allowed over 500 tons on this train on a schedule of 80 minutes for the more than 80 miles to Rugby. There were no other sights quite like them on Britain's railways. Photographs Peter Groom.*

The two LMS diesels 10000 and 10001 on an early trial trip - the period is presumably late 1948.

Crewe North Jubilee 45624 ST. HELENA on a Euston - Bletchley local, 2nd July 1958. This, believe it or not, was a Crewe North turn, and almost anything, including Patriots, could turn up - frequently the locos would be ex-works. Photograph Alec Swain.

*Empty carriage stock was constantly on the move in and out of Euston, with arrivals dragged out from the east side, taken to Camden or Willesden and eventually dragged back. A junior link at Willesden did much of the work and locos turned up on a much more ad hoc basis than at say, Paddington. Apart from the gaggle of clapped out regulars lurking in the sidings beyond the bridges, engines off overnight goods to Broad Street might be set to work, a circumstance which might explain this 8F. 11th August 1956. Photograph A.R. Gault.*

*Euston caught in one of its strange silent interludes, 3rd October 1962. Photograph G.T. Whewly.*

*The drift into Euston; 45733 NOVELTY comes in on 2nd October 1954. Euston's customary gaggle of pilots (see later) is just visible in the distance. Photograph R.C. Riley.*

*The up Merseyside Express entering Euston around 1957/58. Black 5 No.45493 at the head; the train engine is 46200 THE PRINCESS ROYAL. With the headboard on the Pacific, the assumption must be that the 4-6-0's attachment was unlooked for - shortage of steam in the train engine around Rugby maybe? Almost any explanation is possible. Photograph Peter Groom.*

A couple of pages that very much capture the later days of Euston. Left our friend the Merseyside Express again, behind Edge Hill's 46207 PRINCESS ARTHUR OF CONNAUGHT, coming into Euston on 2nd July 1958. Photograph Alec Swain.

8Fs on empty stock work, August 1958.

Euston in August 1963. Jubilee No.45726 INVINCIBLE with an express for Liverpool Lime Street. Right to the platform end and right to the fag end of steam working (such matters lingered on for a while even with more or less full scale dieselisation) Euston maintained the tradition of platform clutter. Jubilees could fair shoot out of Euston like rockets, though these tended to be the Birmingham trains - for it was considered Bushbury men in particular had learned the particular skills required for the three-cylinder 4-6-0s. Photograph C.R.L. Coles.

*Euston on 4th July 1964 and Black 5 No.45418 drifts in with the 7.55 ex-Blackpool. Photograph Alec Swain.*

*The new order - D329 after arrival with the 8.30 ex-Stockport on the same day. Photograph Alec Swain.*

*Last look at the Euston of yore - the fascinating glimpse afforded by one of those peculiarly quiet interludes that we have already seen. It demonstrates how tightly confined and subterranean the site really was and how embankment walls and streets bound the station.*

As we have seen the LMS had been threatening to re-order Euston from the 1930s and a first stab at making the place more workable in modern conditions were alterations to the layout and signalling carried out in 1952. A major fatality was the ancient No.2 signal box which was taken down and replaced by the 'Euston' box, the unattractive but workmanlike flat top brick structure seen earlier boasting the sign "Euston 300 yards", as NOVELTY drifted by. This is 5th October 1952, almost certainly a Sunday with at least two ballast trains full of rails and suchlike and a host of men at work.

Departure signal for platforms 12 and 13. The new signalling at Euston, which involved the first use of the electro-pneumatic system at a main line London terminus, came into use late in 1952. Work had begun in March 1951 on a budget of some £300,000. Far reaching effects on train working were promised but the abolition of 1, 2 and 3 boxes and the main line work previously under control of No.4 would be transferred to the new box, leaving only carriage and engine line movements to be handled by No.4 (renamed Euston Carriage Sidings). The area control extended up to that operated by Camden No.1 box - the track layout had become very complicated over time with eighteen diamond crossings of which eleven had inside or outside slips and two had double slips. Curvature moreover was very sharp in some places leading to heavy wear and tear and difficult maintenance. The two Ampthill Square bridges had always made matters terribly awkward especially in bad weather and as a principal plank of the work the southern-most one was removed, to the great benefit of operations. Inadequate platform length had long been a disadvantage at Euston with up trains frequently standing with their tails foul of connections, preventing others from running to platform lines which would otherwise have been able to receive them. Removal of the southern bridge and the old No.2 box enabled Platforms 1, 2, 3, 6, 7 and 15, by up to 190ft.

Euston colour lights on 16th February 1960, platforms 4 and 5. The great scheme of 1952 had a life of only 13 years, for a new box in connection with the electrification and rebuilding opened in September 1965 on the west side between Cardington Street and Ampthill Square. Some colour lights had been installed in 1935 when platforms 12 and 13 were lengthened to accommodate 15 coach trains and colour lights had been installed on the electric lines between Camden and Watford throughout by 1932 (and on the main lines from Camden to Sudbury in 1943) They were extended from Camden to Euston two years later. Over the years colour lights had also replaced a number of semaphores in the area of the terminus itself.

# CHAPTER FIVE

# GLOOM AND GLORY : DEMISE

The Minister of Transport and Civil Aviation, ensconced in his tower in Berkeley Square, London W1, heard on 19th December 1957 the results of his inspector's examination of the new signalling at Euston:

*"Sir,*
*We have the honour to report for the information of the Minister that, by arrangement with the General Manager, we inspected on 24th November 1957, the new works at Euston station, in the London Midland Region, British Railways. The works comprised the remodelling and simplification of much of the track layout, the lengthening of some platforms and the modernisation of the signalling. The new signal box, which controls all the signalling at the station, was brought into use in 1952, and the work generally was completed in 1955..."*

What follows is an account of the work which fashioned Euston into its final steam age form; the horrors of reconstruction and its ghastly results in the 1960s were as yet unguessed at... The work of the approach layout, which had grown over the years, was much simplified, and this was possible through the removal of the piers of the Ampthill Road overbridge (No.3) and the large No.2 mechanical signal box. The removal of the bridge piers enabled the arrival platform lines and platforms to be lengthened, so avoiding the fouling of the incoming platform connections by long trains.

The lines out of the station ran approximately northwards and after the new work the platform lines from the east side to the west were allocated as follows:-

Nos.1, 2 and 3 – Solely for main line arrivals.

No.4 – Electric arrivals and departures.

No.5 – Electric and steam 'residential' arrivals and departures.

No.6 – Steam 'residential' and main line arrivals and departures.

No.7 – Electric and steam 'residential' arrivals and departures.

No.8 – Parcels.

No.9 – Main line arrivals and departures.

Nos. 10 and 11 – Sidings.

Nos 12 through to 15 – Solely for main line departures.

The departure platforms were reconstructed in 1954, with the loss of one siding, which enabled Nos.13 and 14 platforms to be lengthened at the buffer stop ends. The concourse behind the buffer stops was enlarged and an 'outdoor type of café' (whatever that means) was

arranged under the station roof on the former site of the bookstall. The bookstall was now sited immediately behind the buffer stops of Nos.13 and 14 platforms; it was not a very desirable site, but it was accepted by The Men from the Ministry "in view of the low speed with empty stock arrivals only", and the buffer stops in any case consisted of heavy and solid concrete blocks.

The old timber platforms on the departure side were done away with and the new platforms had pre-cast concrete faces with hard filling and a tarmacadam surface. No.13 platform edge was examined and found to be at the correct height of 3ft. above rail level, but the No.12 platform edge, it transpired, was only 2ft 7½ins. above rail level at the outer end. No.12 platform was slightly higher than the others owing to the general state of the levels of the approach lines and it was found difficult, if not impossible, to lower it. A cross slope on the platform would have been objectionable, and in the circumstances the variation from standard dimensions was accepted. There were some minor divergence of platform lateral clearances, which was also acceptable "in view of the low prevailing speeds and the consequential absence of lurching." The matter was a serious one; lateral clearances of the concave face of No.13 platform had been reduced below the standard to lessen the gap in the centre of a coach, following an accident in which two passengers slipped down between coach and platform, and were injured.

The side clearances from the various bridge piers and abutments and retaining walls were found to be nowhere less than the minimum laid down in the Regulations; where such clearances came near to the minimum they were marked by standard red and white chequer board signs. One of the roof supporting stanchions between No.15 platform line and the adjacent No.19 siding slightly infringed the minimum clearance from the crossover line and this also was marked by a red chequer board sign. So for anyone puzzling over such an object in any photograph, there is the explanation.

The layout of the permanent way at the approaches to the station had grown very complicated in the course of time and the new layout, which for the most part was is in 109lb. flat bottom stuff, was greatly simplified in the course of the work. 'As an instance', the Inspectors recorded, 'the number of diamond crossings has been reduced to 5 from 18 and there are now 2 double slips and 2 single slips compared to 2 and 9 respectively in the former layout.' This was of course extremely clever design work. The standard gauge ballast was overlaid with a layer of ¾in. chippings which served to keep the lower ballast clean; it was shovelled away and renewed when dirty.

The completion of all this work represented at last some sort of return to proper standards after the vicissitudes of war and in general, the track in and around Euston was notable for its high standard of maintenance – especially so under the se-

*Surviving semaphores (replaced by colour lights the next day - see opposite) on Camden Bank 9th June 1945. This book celebrates the Euston of yore and unashamedly ignores the modern station. A similar plea of guilty must be entered for the dc electrics, for although they were a vital and lively enough part of the Euston working, they essentially relate to an entirely new railway, the birth of which was much delayed. The LNW was "preparing for a new railway" for years and it came into force only haltingly. Third and fourth rail electric trains between Euston and Watford began working on 10th July 1922 when Platforms 4, 5 and 7 in the terminus were electrified. Photograph H.C. Casserley.*

**POWER SIGNALLING AT EUSTON, LONDON MIDLAND REGION, BRITISH RAILWAYS 1952**

Courtesy of THE RAILWAY GAZETTE.

## EUSTON S.B.

227 LEVER ALL ELECTRIC POWER FRAME.

187 WORKING.    26 SPARE.    14 SPACES.

SPARES: 6, 18, 28, 34, 52, 56, 73, 74, 83, 91, 102,
117, 121, 157, 158, 164, 171, 172, 188, 199, 204,
205, 206, 217, 219.

SPACES: 75, 76, 77, 144, 145, 146, 147, 148,
149, 150, 151, 152, 153, 154.

GROUND SIGNALS IN THE NORMAL DIRECTION OF RUNNING WILL CLEAR WITH THE
RUNNING SIGNAL IN REAR WITHOUT THE OPERATION OF THEIR INDIVIDUAL LEVERS,
WILL REMAIN "OFF" AFTER REPLACEMENT OF THE RUNNING SIGNAL LEVER AND
WILL BE REPLACED TO DANGER IN SEQUENCE BY TRACK CIRCUIT
EMERGENCY REPLACEMENT BY PULLING AND REPLACING THE RELEVANT GROUND
SIGNAL LEVER.

vvvv  ELECTRIFIED LINES WITH THIRD AND FOURTH RAILS.

TRACK SECTION 5517 IS COVERED BY AXLE COUNTING WITHOUT TRACK CIRCUIT.

──────  ELECTRICAL DEPRESSION BAR.

G.F. RELEASE 27
(1) RELEASE LEVER AND F.P.L.
(1) POINTS

F.P.L. (1) NORMALLY IN

AXLE COUNTING TREADLE

G.F. RELEASE 115
(1) RELEASE LEVER
(1)(3)(4) POINTS
(5) SLOT ON INCOMING SIGNALS

FIELD SIDINGS

HORSE BOX LINE

IRISH MAIL LINE

N° 1 PLATFORM
N° 2
N° 3
N° 4
N° 5
N° 6
N° 7
N° 8 PLATFORM
N° 9
N° 10
N° 11
SIDING N° 10
SIDING N° 11
BRAKE PIT ROAD
N° 12 PLATFORM
N° 13
ROAD N° 2
N° 14
N° 15
SIDING N° 18
N° 19

STANDS ON GROUND
ADJACENT TO DERAILER

REFUELLING SIDINGS

SLOTTED FROM EUSTON
CARRIAGE SIDINGS S.B.

UP SIDE CARRIAGE
SHED 0.F.

DOWN EMPTY CARRIAGE LINE

UP ENGINE LINE N° 2

UP FAST
UP SLOW
DOWN FAST

UP ENGINE LINE N° 1

UP FAST →
UP SLOW →
← DOWN SLOW
← DOWN FAST

BACKING OUT ROAD N° 1
UP ENGINE LINE N° 1 →

A
B
C
D

OPERATED BY PLUNGER AT SIGNAL
AND WHEN THAT SIGNAL IS "OFF"
TO OTHER THAN REFUELLING
SIDINGS

WORKED FROM EUSTON
CARRIAGE SIDINGS S.B.

(181) TO BACKING OUT ROAD N° 1
(182)  "    "    "    "    " 2
(183)  "    "    "    "    " 3
(184)  "    "    "    "    " 4

CAMDEN N° 1 UP STARTING SIGNALS

UP FAST →
UP SLOW →
← DOWN SLOW
← DOWN FAST

EUSTON CARRIAGE
SIDINGS UP STARTING
SIGNAL

CAMDEN N° 1 DOWN OUTER HOME SIGNALS

From Watford

vere conditions prevailing at the approaches to a heavily worked terminus. The alignment, 'top' and cross levels left little to be desired, and the LMR Assistant Chief Civil Engineer declared that a special check had been made of the gauge throughout the layout on the day before the BOT inspection. Except on one of the departure lines on to which 'a large quantity of provisions had been deposited', evidently from a dining car, the whole appearance of the layout was neat and tidy and was a credit to the Permanent Way Inspector and the maintenance gang, who 'must be discouraged' the Inspectors felt, 'by such thoughtless actions on the part of other staff.'

An exception to the good general standard of maintenance of the track was found – the wet and dirty condition of the formation at the 'gathering' of the departure platform lines where engines stood at the head of outgoing trains in the neighbourhood of overbridge No.4. The problem was also noticeable in the dip where the Down Fast line and the connecting line to the backing out roads passed under overbridge No.5. In view of the low speeds, however, the safety of traffic was not affected by these conditions; the BOT appreciated the difficulty in keeping ballast clean with oil and water dripping from standing engines but recorded that such wet and dirty places were 'an undesirable blemish on otherwise thoroughly well maintained track work, and we hope that they will receive early attention.'

The extent of the work to be carried out at Euston station had not been finally decided when the new colour light signalling between Camden and Sudbury Junction was brought into use in 1945-1946. In consequence the manual semaphore signalling of Euston itself and its immediate approaches had been allowed to remain 'for the time being' with very little track circuiting. The new power operated signal box, with complete track circuiting and colour light signalling, was brought into use in October 1952, but in the meantime some track circuiting had been installed on the departure lines, as a result of a collision which occurred on 6th August 1949, when a long empty train was backed by mistake into an occupied platform.

The new installation was by 2, 3, and 4-aspect multi-lens colour light running signals and position light subsidiary and shunting signals. Theatre type route indicators were used. The running signals were well sited and the clarity of the signalling 'immeasurably superior' to that of the old installation, making the task of drivers, particularly of incoming trains, much simpler. A minor criticism concerned the single yellow light of the Up Fast home signal No.7, which was not very well focused for a distant view on the left handed

*Old for New. Excellent illustrations of replacement work in and around Euston on 16th September 1952. Certainly, some wonderful little signals disappeared.*

curve. This was afterwards adjusted to the requirements of the BOT. The points were operated electro pneumatically. There was complete track circuiting throughout the layout, controlled, in general, quite conventionally.*

The new signal box was a substantial brick and concrete structure on the Up side of the line just north of overbridge No.5; it had two floors, the upper being the working floor and the lower accommodating the large relay room. A smaller building close by housed the electrically worked air compressors for the electro pneumatic point operation, together with standby diesel engine generator and compressor. The new signal box replaced the following old boxes:-

(a) The main No.2 box formerly situated in the approximate centre of the approach layout close to the ends of the platforms.

(b) No.1 box (the 'bell box') at the buffer stop ends of the arrival platforms, and

(c) No.3 box at the south end of the backing out roads. No.4 box from hereon no longer took any part in the signalling of the main running lines but was retained for working the carriage sidings, and renamed accordingly.

Train describer working was put in force between the new box and Camden No.1 box over the continuously track circuited lines, although block working was retained over the continuously track circuited lines north of Camden No.1. The installation was worked by a miniature lever frame (from the Westinghouse Brake and Signal Company) originally intended for the resignalling of Preston before the war, but adapted for Euston. It boasted 191 working levers, electrically interlocked, in one continuous row. The levers had 'a smooth working action and the finish of the frame, and in fact of the box generally, (was) excellent.'

There was no indication check locking on the point levers, but points were indicated 'N' and 'R' behind their levers, and all the aspects of the running signals were indicated behind their respective levers. Ground signals were indicated by two horizontal or two diagonal white lights. The train describers were arranged conventionally on a shelf above the levers, together with the telephone instruments which communicated with the telephones at selected running signals. There were also 'Train Running Away' indicators, which referred to the Up inner and outer homes and the Down starting signals.

The track circuiting was indicated by two identical diagrams, one at each end of the long frame, and they were considered, for the day, to be remarkably clear and distinct 'without any lateral overcrowding

of the track line.' Included on the diagrams were pairs of yellow bullseye lights at the ends of the platforms, illuminated by the station staff when a train was ready to start; a bell rang at the same time in the signal box. The lighting of the working floor of the new Euston box, by vapour discharge, was 'very good' and (it comes as a surprise to us now) the fact that it could be 'dimmed at will by the signalman' was considered a great advance.

The box was also well equipped with linemen's working and mess rooms, lavatories, etc. and the large relay room was 'very well arranged with all metal shelves and detachable top relays.' The wiring was of the 'flame-proof' type, and a battery of carbon dioxide cylinders discharged automatically through 'orifices on the walls and ceiling' in the event of smoke or a rise in the ambient temperature. This was presumably the forerunner of sprinkler systems. 'Ample provision' was made for 'holding the road' by the occupation of successive track circuits after a signal had been cleared. Special track circuit control

applied to the incoming call-on signals on the running lines and backing out carriage sidings, went a long way to ensure that a train could not be admitted to a platform at which there was not room to receive it. This control was first applied at Liverpool Lime Street when that station was resignalled in 1948.

The new Euston box was manned normally by 'a regulator' and three signalmen at the frame, but on Sundays there was a regulator and only two signalmen on duty. The new works involved in this extensive remodelling and resignalling scheme were in the opinion of the BOT of "first class construction, complete and in good order, and they reflect credit on all those responsible for their conception, design and execution."

---

*Full descriptions of the installation were given in a booklet prepared by the Signal Engineer, with much of it repeated in articles in 'Engineering' and 'The Engineer' published, for those with a technical bent and the necessary access, in October 1952.*

*16th September 1952 - No.2 box when built contained 288 levers, which replaced one of 54. Each frame had 144 levers arranged in the centre with the signalmen face to face. In March 1906 the original frames of F.W. Webb's tumbler action type with direct lever locking were replaced by two others arranged in the windows, this time with the men working back to back. These were of the catch-handle pattern, with ordinary tappet locking, introduced by A.M. Thompson, then the Signal Superintendent. The position of the outside connections had necessarily to remain the same so the levers in these new frames were numbered right to left (the reverse of normal practice) keeping the same numbers to the same functions. The Euston - Camden widening came in the early years of the century giving four running roads to Camden with a subway under the departure lines, so empty stock from incoming trains could reach carriage sidings without blocking departure roads.*

16th September 1952 and the exterior of the great No.2 box. The bridge confining it at the southern end has been removed - see the picture page 23 for an idea of how shoehorned it was between the two overbridges.

Inside the old No.2 box, 16th September 1952. It dated from 1891 and was certainly showing its age. At the time of its construction it was the largest in the country and "probably in the world". Its chronic defect was always its location between the two overbridges.

The work in progress, 3rd October 1952. The bare brickwork delineates the former site of the second, southern-most bridge - now gone. Even as a modernising signal installation took place there was still a fabulous amount of detail on the 1950s steam railway - cables, lamp posts and masts, fencing, hoarded crossings, water

The end approaches - above - the work of lengthening the platforms probably caused more disruption than the replacement of the box, and some trains were stopped short of Euston; others diverted to St. Pancras, whilst boat trains from Liverpool ran into Paddington. Certain newspaper and parcels trains also departed from Maiden Lane instead of Euston. Below - carrying off the bones of the carcass.

*Down into the maw of Euston, 30th October 1952. 3F tank taking water: this would probably be the up side carriage pilot (refer to the signal diagram for position of the siding). This was the last set of main line arrival signals with route indicators at the approach to Euston.*

*The new box was hardly an architectural triumph - this is the view looking north. It was built to the specifications of Mr. S. Williams, the regional S & T engineer and there was a special press inspection on October 2nd 1952. The new box had two floors, a relay room below and an operating room above, with a Westinghouse 'L' frame of 227 levers. The interlocking was all electric and about 350 routes were controlled by the frame.*

*The new box on 22nd June 1953. The new work was commissioned in stages and for this all points which were to be retained in the new layout were converted to electro-pneumatic operation to be worked temporarily from their levers in the old No.2 and No.3 boxes. The new connections were laid in and clipped wherever possible so that alterations could be made when No.2 box had been closed and removed. From the proliferation of VIROL adverts, the stuff might well have kept the enamel sign industry going singlehandedly. What happened to it?*

*The lever frame in the new box, 1st October 1952.*

*Classic shot of an ascent up Camden Bank, a capable Royal Scot No.6165 THE RANGER (12th LONDON REGT.) with banker at the rear.*

# CAMDEN BANK AND SHED

*As soon as the new box was at work Platforms 6 to 10 closed to traffic, the old box was cleared away and the new lines and platform extensions put in as rapidly as possible. Platforms 3 and 4 were next closed for similar work and in two further stages the whole station was open for service again - the whole operation occupied approximately five weeks. The power lever frame was original provided by Westinghouse Brake and Signal Company in connection with an installation to be made at Preston but this was not proceeded with, the equipment transferring to Euston.*

*Classic E.R. Wethersett photograph, subject for the V. Welch painting and inspi-*
*ration for man and boy alike ever since. This is Camden Bank 23rd September*
*1938. Streamlined 6221 QUEEN ELIZABETH is on the down Coronation passing*
*Euston Carriage Sidings box, a Jubilee 5563 AUSTRALIA is backing out on the*
*down empty carriage line. Photograph E.R. Wethersett.*

*E.R. Wethersett again and Patriot 5525 COLWYN BAY.*

*Camden Bank 9th June 1945. It is a well recorded place - Camden shed lay alongside and its frequent visitors could easily take in the main line as well. Pacifics await to descend to the terminus on the right - engines could go down in cavalcade. Photograph H.C. Casserley.*

The Euston pilots were something of an institution in themselves. Apart from a 3F tank or so from Camden shunting the station itself, the successive generations of engines responsible for the empty carriage stock were almost exclusively in the hands of Willesden. They lurked outside like a flock of chickens at roosting time and it was traditional over many decades (despite the formidable qualities of the bank) for elderly, the end in sight, locos to be used. All these pictures were taken on 4th May 1946, a period when strangely enough ex-Midland 2F 0-6-0s found favour. Photograph H.C. Casserley.

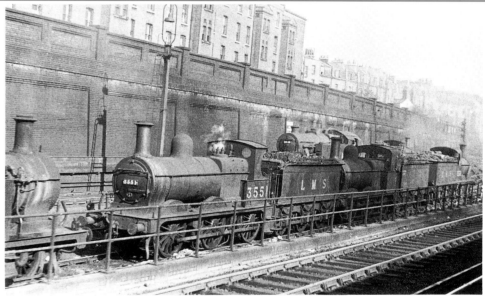

3551, 3014 and 3536 outside Euston on 4th May 1946. With the 2Fs had come a clear out of the creaking ex-LNW types previously on the task, though the 0-6-0s were not obviously better in any particular respect. Photograph H.C. Casserley.

The 2Fs gave way to all sorts - 2-6-2 tanks, 8Fs and latterly 78XXX Moguls - all manner of locos in effect. The outside foreman at Willesden would eagerly seek out an engine for the pilot gang which had a steam heat pipe on the front, vital for heating purposes and invaluable in eking out the supply of locos. Photograph H.C. Casserley.

*Thompson designed L1 2-6-4 tank, one of a couple on a brief and unsuccessful trial from the Eastern Region, 21st September 1958. Photograph R.C. Riley.*

*Patriot 5541 DUKE OF SUTHERLAND at the top of Camden Bank, 9th June 1945. Photograph H.C. Casserley.*

*Roaring progress over the empty carriage and engine lines, 7th July 1954, with 46114 COLDSTREAM GUARDSMAN.*

The Bank in the 1930s and an almost awesome look up to 6201 PRINCESS ELIZABETH at full pelt - banker at rear.
Photograph C.R.L. Coles.

Furrowed brows, lit fags and caps pushed back outside Euston, 42121 resolutely derailed 12th May 1950. Photograph H.C. Casserley.

*The quintessential Camden Bank - an LNWR portrait as fine as any likely to be found anywhere.*

*The down Manxman in the charge of 46164 THE ARTIST'S RIFLEMAN; just passed Camden engine shed, the train is marching up to Primrose Hill tunnels. Below is the Down Watford, next to it the Up.*

*The up Ulster Express behind ROYAL SCOT on the flyover at the crest of the bank, 7th July 1954. Behind is Camden No.2 box; down below are the two dc lines, the Down breaking away to the left.*

*Primrose Hill, 21st July 1951. 4F 4397 on empty stock on the Up Slow, a Caprotti 4-6-0 on the siding. The view is from above the Primrose Hill tunnel portal - 44749 is on the dead end siding which (left) takes it to Camden Goods, (right) to the north yard of Camden shed. On the right, hard against the retaining wall, is the Down Fast, and alongside it the Up Fast. On the far left against the wall the line eventually leads down the subway; in the right middle distance (behind the box) is the Camden locomen's dorm - the 'barracks'. Photograph H.C. Casserley.*

*Patriot 45516 on the bank passes the "smoky claustrophobia" of Camden shed on 6th July 1958. The train is a Sunday express from Euston to Northampton and Stafford and the pre-occupied group beyond are members of the Railway Photographic Society. The gentleman in the Mackintosh with the tripod is the late Maurice Earley, to the left in a blazer is Geoff Rixon, chatting to Lewis Coles. Photograph and caption by Brian Morrison.*

*45709 IMPLACABLE tops Camden Bank with the 4.35pm express for Birmingham in 1958. THE PRINCESS ROYAL off Edge Hill backs into the shed having arrived at Euston earlier with an express from Liverpool. Photograph Brian Morrison.*

*The classic line up shown in the background opposite. From left to right, Black 5 44942, 46238 CITY OF CARLISLE and rebuilt Patriot 45528, all coaled and ready for backing down to Euston. This was the sort of transfixing sight that greeted the visitor to Camden, a tiny cramped, smoky and cluttered shed groaning with the very mightiest of West Coast steam power. Photograph Brian Morrison.*

*Camden on 28th May 1960, CITY OF CARLISLE close by the ash pits. Photograph Peter Groom.*

*Caprotti Black 5 from Longsight - 44752 alongside 45412 all the way from Carlisle, 1958. Photograph Brian Morrison.*

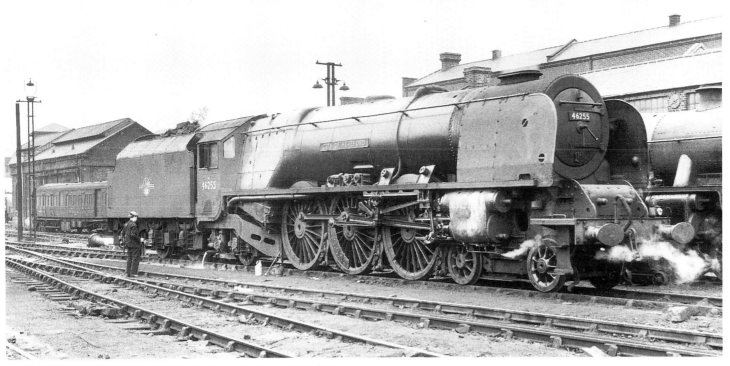

*CITY OF HEREFORD in 1958. Photograph Brian Morrison.*

*Sad decline. Steam locomotives were cleared out of Camden shed by 1964 and large tracts of the roof simply removed for the new order to stand open to the elements. That part to the right had some years before been converted into a diesel maintenance shop and retained its covering. The whole lot was demolished a few months later but this May 1964 view still shows the Camden goods traffic at a healthy level.*

*Going out on a high note. 45546 FLEETWOOD on the 70ft vacuum operated Camden turntable, 1958. Photograph Brian Morrison.*